Visual QuickStart Guide

PageMaker 4 for the Macintosh

Tony Webster
Carrie Webster

○ Peachpit Press

Visual QuickStart Guide:
PageMaker 4 for the Macintosh
Tony Webster Carrie Webster

Peachpit Press, Inc.
2414 Sixth Street
Berkeley, CA 94710
(415) 548-4393
(415) 548-5991 (fax)

First Edition published 1991

ISBN: 0-938151-71-1

0 9 8 7 6 5 4 3 2 1
Printed and bound in the United States

Why a Visual QuickStart?

Virtually no one actually reads computer books; rather, people typically refer to them. This series of **Visual QuickStart Guides** has made that reference easier thanks to a new approach to learning computer applications.

While conventional computer books lean towards providing extensive textual explanations, a **Visual QuickStart Guide** takes a far more visual approach—pictures literally show you what to do, and text is limited to clear, concise commentary. Learning becomes easier, because a **Visual QuickStart** familiarizes you with the look and feel of your software. Learning also becomes faster, since there are no long-winded passages to comb through.

It's a new approach to computer learning, but it's also solidly based on experience: Webster & Associates have logged thousands of hours of classroom computer training, and have authored several books on desktop publishing topics.

Chapter 1 provides an overview of how to install PageMaker 4 and the general method of operation.

Chapters 2 through **15** graphically overview the major PageMaker features; these chapter are easy to reference and, with the extensive use of screen shots, allow concepts to be quickly grasped.

Chapter 16 provides an overall menu summary, explaining every Page-Maker menu and command.

Appendix A is a roadmap to PageMaker's convenient, time-saving keyboard shortcuts.

Acknowledgments

The authors wish to acknowledge the assistance of Paul Webster and Barbara Larter in writing, laying out and editing this book.

Contents

GETTING STARTED

INSTALLATION SUMMARY

Installing PageMaker 4 is a relatively simple operation. If you
follow the instructions below, you will be installing all
PageMaker files, including all example files. If you do not wish
to install all these files, you may skip the relevant steps below.

INSTALLATION STEPS

Step 1. Insert Disk # 1 into your
Macintosh disk drive.

   When Disk 1 is active it will
contain the different files as
shown here.

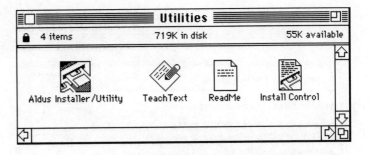

Step 2. Double-click on the *Aldus
Installer/Utility* icon to activate the
Aldus Installer Main Window
dialog box.

   In the *Aldus Installer Main
Window* dialog box, you will
notice that all options for file
installation are crossed. Here you
must de-select which files you do
not wish to install.

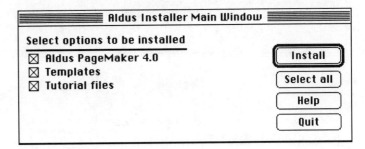

Step 3. De-select the options you
do not wish to install, then select
Install.

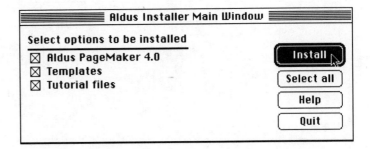

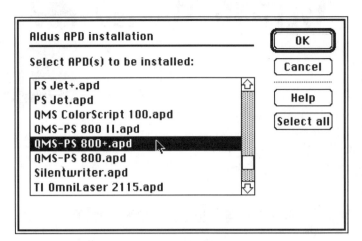

This activates the *Aldus APD Installation* dialog box, where you must select which printer type you will be printing to.

Step 4. Select a printer type or types and select OK.

Use the shift key for multiple selections, or choose *Select all* for all options.

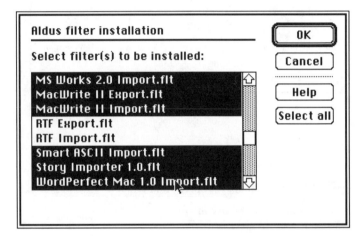

This activates the *Aldus filter installation* dialog box, where you must select a filter or file type for placing of any text files from a word processor into PageMaker.

Step 5. Select a filter or filters and click on OK.

Use the shift key for multiple selections or choose *Select all* for all options. It is recommended to install Smart ASCII Import.flt as well as any other word processor programs you are using.

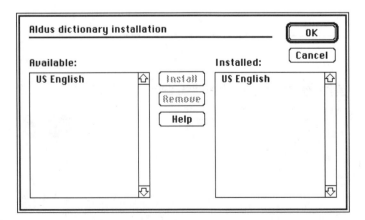

After clicking on OK, the *Aldus dictionary installation* dialog box will be activated. This is where you can select any dictionaries that have been installed on your Macintosh. You may only have one available.

Step 6. Select a dictionary option (if required) and click on OK.

This will activate a dialog box that requires you to personalize PageMaker by entering your name, company and serial number.

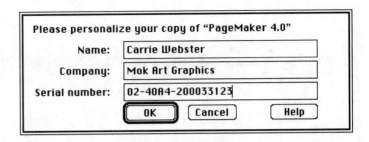

Step 7. Enter your name, company and serial number details, and click on OK.

The serial number is found on the bottom of the PageMaker 4 box, or on the registration card in the package.

Clicking on OK will activate the confirmation dialog box.

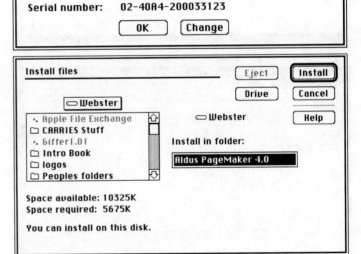

Step 8. Click on OK if your details are correct.

This will activate the *Install files* dialog box.

Step 9. Specify where you would like PageMaker 4 to be installed on your hard disk and select Install.

Search through the folders on the hard disk for the folder in which you would like to locate PageMaker.

After you select Install. PageMaker will now prompt you to install the disks as they are required.

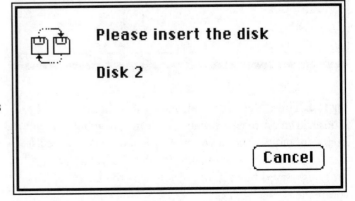

Step 10. Install disks 2, 3 and 4 as prompted by the screen.

Once completed, the Install program will bring you back to the Macintosh desktop, ready to start using PageMaker 4.

Starting PageMaker

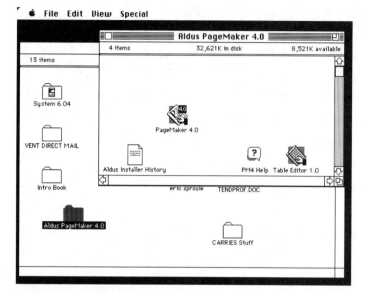

Figure 1. Activating PageMaker 4 is a matter of locating the PageMaker 4 icon on the desktop and double-clicking on it. This icon will be located inside the Aldus PageMaker 4.0 folder wherever you have placed it on the hard disk.

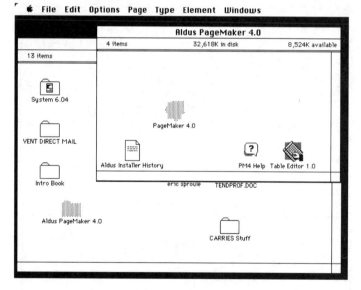

Figure 2. Once PageMaker has opened, your screen will be similar to the one shown here. At this point you have the choice of creating a new publication, or opening a previously saved publication. Both of these operations are performed through the **File** menu.

Figure 3. This is the **File** menu, activated by holding the mouse down on the word **File**. To create a new publication, keep your mouse held down, move the mouse down the list and release it on the command *New*. Similarly, you open a previously-saved publication, by selecting the *Open* command.

PAGE SETUP

Figure 4. The *Page setup* dialog box is now activated, which allows you to define attributes on how your publication will look. We will be changing dialog box options in Chapter 2, **Setting up a Publication**. For now, click the mouse once on the word OK. This action will bring you into a new PageMaker publication, as shown in Figure 5.

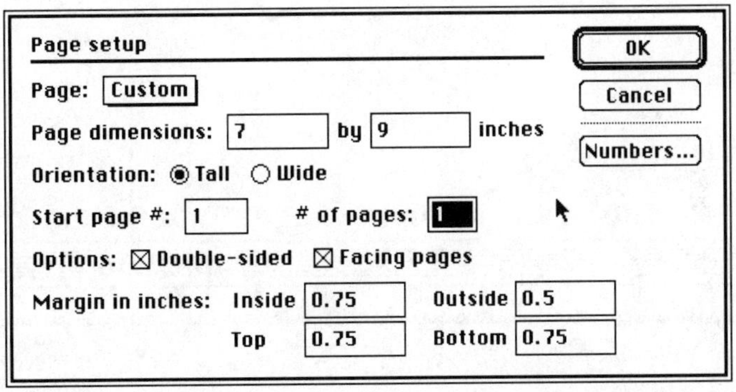

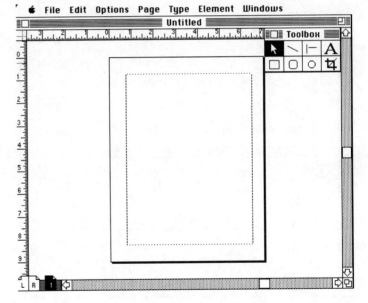

Figure 5. After selecting OK in the *Page setup* dialog box, this is how a new Untitled publication will look.

THE PAGEMAKER SCREEN

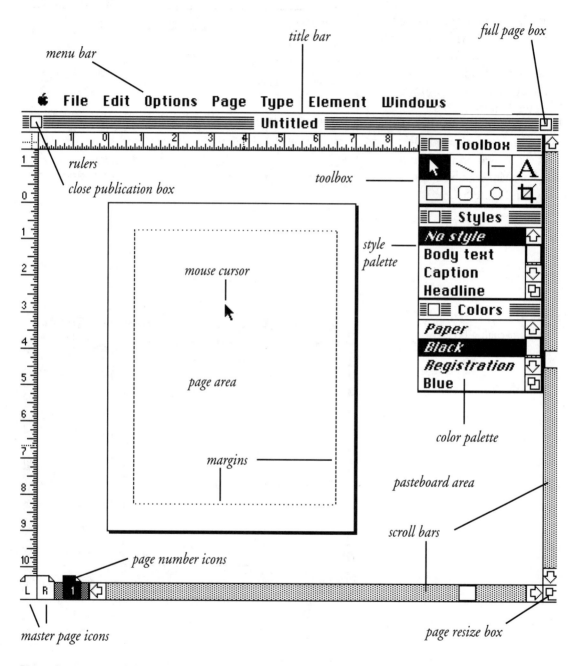

Figure 6. The PageMaker screen. Your screen may not contain all these components when you first turn on PageMaker.

SCREEN COMPONENTS

Menu bar

Figure 7. Clicking on any name in the **menu bar** produces a series of drop-down menu commands for operating PageMaker.

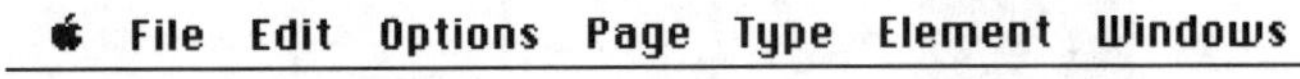

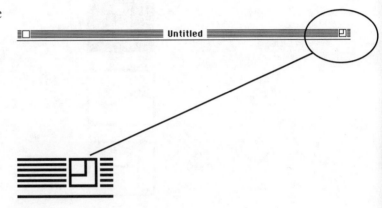

Title bar

Figure 8. The **title bar** contains the name of the PageMaker publication. If it has not yet been given a name, it will read **Untitled**.

Full page box

Figure 9. This box is used to resize the PageMaker window, if it does not fill the screen.

Rulers

Figure 10. The **rulers** are used to measure distance on the screen. Ruler guides can be dragged from the rulers. The measurement units can be changed, and the zero point can be moved to any area on the screen

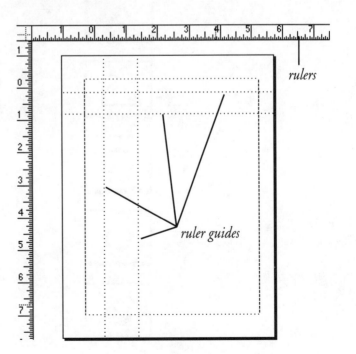

Ruler guides

Ruler guides are non-printing guides that are dragged by the mouse onto the page, from either of the rulers. You can place as many ruler guides on the page as you like, and they can also be moved with the mouse once they have been positioned.

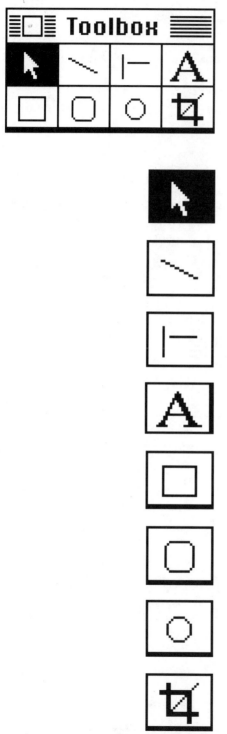

Toolbox

Figure 11. The **toolbox** contains a number of tools that you work with to manipulate, create, resize and move text and graphics on the screen.

The **pointer tool** is used for selecting, moving and resizing text and graphics on the page.

The **diagonal line drawing tool** is used to draw straight lines of any angle on the page.

The **perpendicular line drawing tool** is used for drawing lines at 45 degree increments.

The **text tool** is used for text editing, applying attributes to text, and creating text files.

The **rectangle drawing tool** is used for drawing squares and rectangles.

The **rounded-corner drawing tool** is used for drawing squares and rectangles with rounded corners.

The **ellipse tool** is used for drawing circles and ellipses.

The **cropping tool** is used for cropping imported graphic files.

Close publication box

Figure 12. This box can be used as one way of closing the current PageMaker publication.

Style palette

Figure 13. The **style palette** is used to apply styles to paragraphs of text.

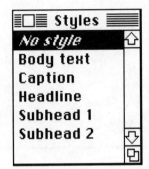

Mouse cursor

Figure 14. The **mouse cursor** is the icon that allows you to move around the screen, corresponding to mouse movement. The shape of the cursor will change depending upon options selected within PageMaker.

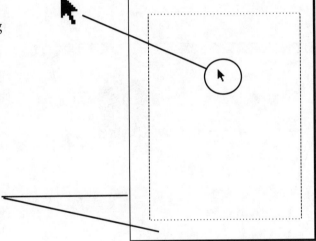

Page area

Figure 15. This area represents your page and its boundaries.

Color palette

Figure 16. The **color palette** is used to apply color to selected text or graphic areas on the screen.

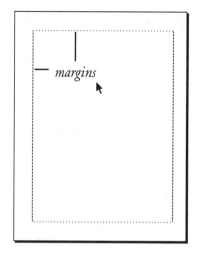

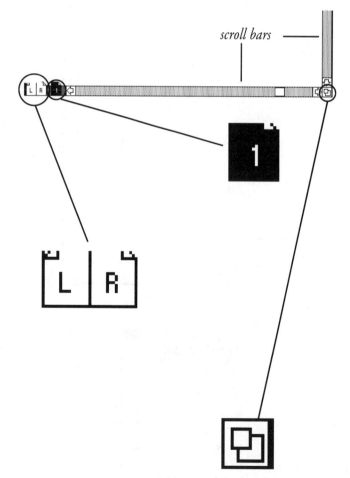

margins

scroll bars

Margins
Figure 17. These are non-printing guides that indicate the defined margins.

Pasteboard area
Figure 18. This is like a desk around your page that can be used to place text or graphics. Any object on the pasteboard will be saved with the publication.

Scroll bars
Figure 19. These are used for moving around the screen to show different parts of your page.

Page number icons
Figure 20. These indicate how many pages are in your publication, and which page you are currently viewing.

Master page icons
Figure 21. Clicking on these icons allows you to access the master pages in your publication. It is possible to have left and right master pages, or just a right master page for a single-sided document.

Page resize box
Figure 22. This box allows you to resize the screen with the mouse.

OPERATING MENUS

Figure 23. To activate a menu, hold the mouse down on the required menu name in the menu bar, and a list of options will appear below the name.

Move the mouse down the list of options, highlight the option you would like and release the mouse.

Three things may happen after selecting a menu command:

Figure 24. a) A dialog box will be activated. Using dialog boxes is explained in the next section.

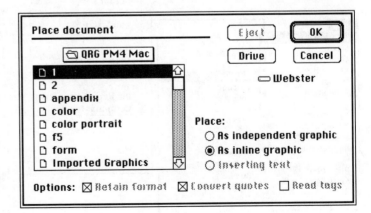

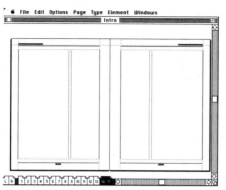

Figure 25. b) An immediate change will occur on the screen, for example, the rulers will disappear, or...

Figure 26. c) The command will not become apparent until a specific action is taken. For example, the *Lock guides* command will lock any ruler and column guides so they cannot be moved by the mouse. This will only be apparent if you try to move a guide with the mouse.

DIFFERENT TYPES OF MENU COMMANDS

Figure 27. Menu commands with ticks appearing to the left of them indicate that this option has been activated. To deactivate any of these commands, click on them with the mouse.

Menu commands ending with three dots will always activate a dialog box.

Menu commands with letters to the right, indicate there is a keyboard shortcut to activate this option.

Figure 28. Menu commands, with an arrow head to the right, have an associated sub-menu which is used in the same way as the main menu.

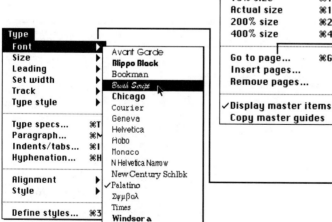

WORKING WITH DIALOG BOXES

Figure 29. This dialog box is activated from the *Type specs* command in the **Type** menu.

There are a number of ways to change options within dialog boxes such as this one.

a) Any option with a box to the left of it can be selected or deselected with the mouse. These are called check boxes, and any number of these may be select-ed in a group.

b) Any button option with three dots after it will activate another dialog box.

Figure 30. c) You can activate a sub-menu from any options contained in a rectangle. Simply hold your mouse down on the rectangle.

Figure 31. d) For numeric options, either double-click inside the box and type in the new value, or click inside the box, backspace over the current value, and type in the new value.

e) Options with circles to the left of them may be selected with a click of the mouse. These are called radio buttons, and only one in a group may be selected.

Use the tab key as one way of moving around dialog boxes such as this.

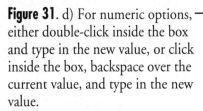

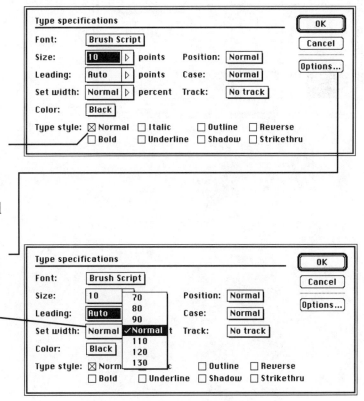

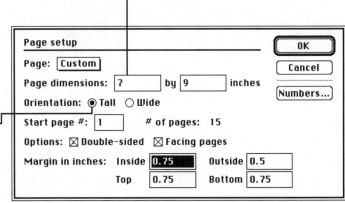

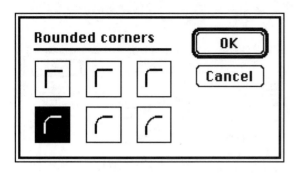

Figure 32. f) Some dialog boxes will display graphic options which can be clicked on with the mouse. The one in reverse video is currently selected.

SETTING UP A PUBLICATION

NEW OR EXISTING PUBLICATIONS

After activating the PageMaker program, you may either create a new publication, or open an existing publication.

NEW PUBLICATION

Figure 1. To start a new publication, select *New* from the File menu, which will activate the *Page setup* dialog box. In this dialog box you can set up page size, orientation, number of pages, double or single-sided, margin values, and page numbering options.

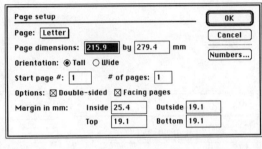

OPENING AN EXISTING PUBLICATION

Figure 2. To open an existing publication, select *Open* from the File menu to activate the *Open publication* dialog box. In this dialog box, you have access to all folders and drives on the hard disk, including the floppy drive. Make your selection and click on OK.

PageMaker publications can also be opened by double-clicking on them while at the Macintosh desktop.

PLACING FILES

Figure 3. The *Place* command from the **File** menu is used to load all types of files into new and existing PageMaker publications — text and/or graphics. Selecting this command activates the Figure 4 dialog box.

Figure 4. The *Place document* command dialog box for loading text or graphics allows you to move around your hard disk to find the necessary file, as is standard for all Macintosh software.

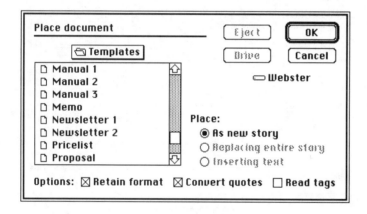

PLACING TEXT FILES

Figure 5. The options for text placement are contained in the *Place document* command dialog box. The options at the bottom include *Retain format* (from wp level), *Convert quotes* (turning wp quotes into typesetting quotes) and *Read tags* (dis-cussed in the **Style Sheets** chapter).

The options at the bottom right are *As new story* (default condition for a new story), *Replacing entire story* (allows selected story to be replaced by the new text) and *Inserting text* (allows new text to be inserted at an insertion point in current text).

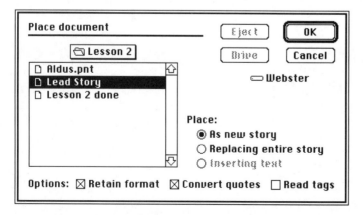

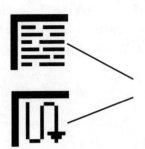

AUTO AND MANUAL TEXT FLOW

Figure 6. By clicking on a text file name and choosing OK, using the *Place document* dialog box, you will return back to the screen with a mouse cursor in one of two modes:

(a) Manual text flow (default setting), or
(b) Automatic text flow

Manual text flow allows text to load into a column (or page—if single column) and then stop. Automatic text flow loads all text into as many columns or pages that are required, creating the pages as they are needed.

Figure 7. Once the mouse cursor changes to a loaded text cursor as shown here, the text can then flow onto the page. Position the cursor where you want the text to start and click the mouse button once.

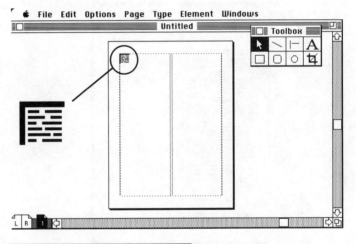

Figure 8. Manual text flow gives us this result; the text flows down column one and then stops. If no text is left to flow, the windowshade handle (see figure) at the bottom will be empty. In this figure it has a down-arrow symbol in it, indicating more text is available.

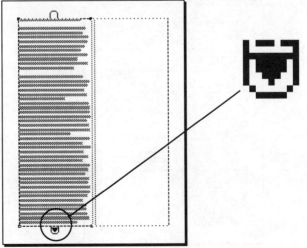

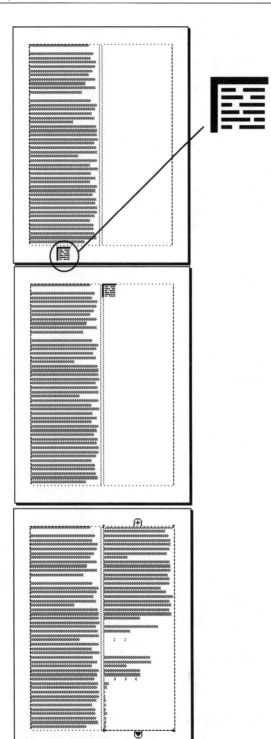

Figure 9. To access the additional text, click the mouse on the down arrow symbol, and the loaded text cursor re-appears.

Figure 10. Position the loaded text cursor at the top of the next column (or wherever you wish to place the text), and click again. The text will now flow down this column and stop at the bottom (even if more text is available).

Figure 11. Repeat the above two figures on additional pages until text runs out. The text file is finished when the bottom windowshade handle is empty.

Options

Rulers	⌘R
Snap to rulers	⌘[
Zero lock	
✓**Guides**	⌘J
✓**Snap to guides**	⌘U
Lock guides	
Column guides...	
Autoflow	
Index entry...	⌘;
Show index...	
Create index...	
Create TOC...	

Figure 12. Automatic text flow allows text to flow across as many columns and pages as necessary to complete the loading of the text file. This mode is activated by choosing *Autoflow* from the **Options** menu. A tick alongside the *Autoflow* command indicates that automatic text flow is turned on.

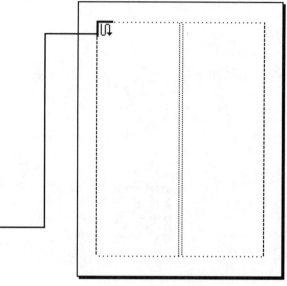

Figure 13. Selecting the *Place* command when in *Autoflow* mode, changes the cursor to the automatic text flow icon, once a text file is selected as shown in Figure 5, and you click on OK to return to the screen. Clicking once in this mode allows the text to flow continuously until finished. Extra pages are automatically generated, if required.

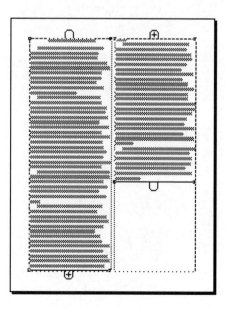

Figure 14. Semi-automatic text flow is achieved by holding down the shift key before you click the mouse cursor in manual or automatic modes. The cursor changes to the semi-automatic text flow as shown here. Text flows down the column (or page) and is already loaded to flow again, without having to click in the bottom windowshade handle first (as discussed in Figure 9).

PLACING GRAPHIC FILES

Figure 15. PageMaker can place a variety of graphics types including: (a) *bitmap*, (b) *object oriented*, (c) *scanned image* , (d) *PostScript*. The different icons that appear for these different graphic types are shown here.

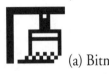 (a) Bitmap

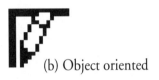 (b) Object oriented

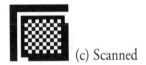 (c) Scanned

 (d) PostScript

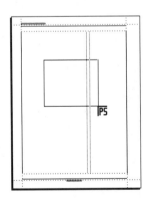

Figure 16. Graphics are loaded the same way as text. Activate the *Place* command, select the graphic file, and place the cursor where you want the graphic to go, and click once.

Unfortunately, this may cause the graphic to appear on the page at an unknown size. It is better to do what is shown here. Draw an imaginary box with the mouse button held down, and then release the mouse. The graphic will appear in the defined area. For more details on placing external graphics, see Chapter 6.

COLUMN AND MARGIN GUIDES

Figure 17. You may adjust the number of columns through the *Column guides* command in the **Options** menu. This invokes the *Column guides* dialog box. In our dialog box, we have changed the number of columns to 3.

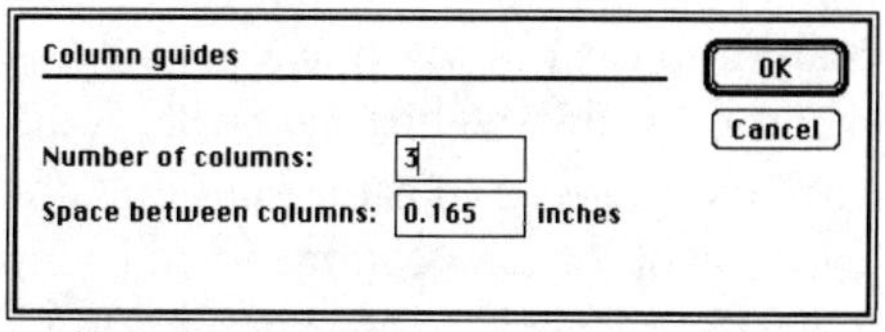

Figure 18. If text is already placed on a page, changing the number of columns does not alter its layout. This text must be manually resized with the mouse, or deleted and re-flowed onto the page.

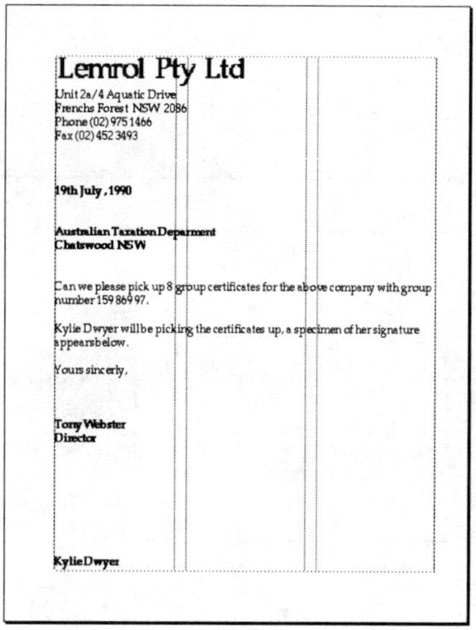

Note: Margins are setup initially in the New dialog box, and modified in the Page setup dialog box as discussed earlier in this chapter.

Figure 19. You can manually change margin and column guides on the screen. Position the mouse on the column guide or margin, hold the mouse down, and reposition the margin or column guide; then release the mouse.

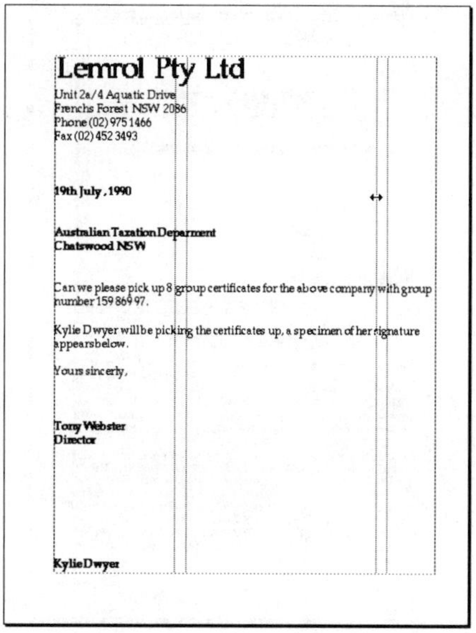

SAVING PUBLICATIONS

Figure 20. Once text and or graphics files are loaded, the publication can be saved using the *Save* command in the **File** menu. Initially, the first *Save* will produce the *Save as* dialog box, allowing you to name your document. Subsequent selection of the *Save* command will simply save to disk any new changes made to your publication.

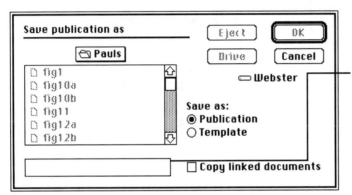

Figure 21. The *Save as* dialog box allows you to type a name for the publication, in the rectangle in the bottom left corner of the box. As for most Macintosh applications, you can first choose the folder and disk in which to save the file.

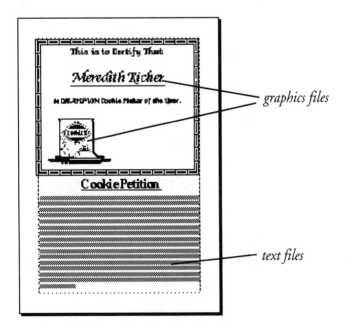

graphics files

text files

LINKING FILES

Figure 22. Text and graphics files within PageMaker can be automatically linked to their original external files. This allows PageMaker publications to be automatically updated if the external files are modified.

Figure 23. The *Links* command from the **File** menu gives access to the *Links* dialog box (Figure 24).

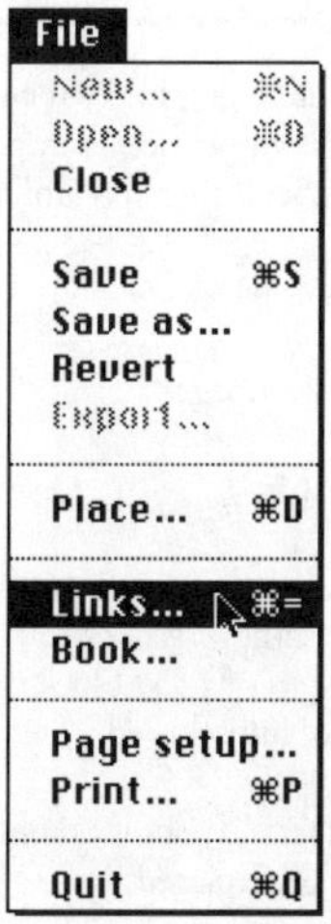

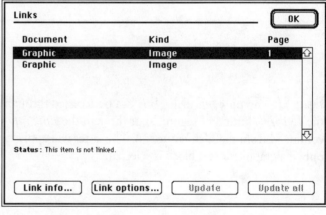

Figure 24. The *Links* dialog box. Selecting a file from this dialog box gives the current file status. The *Update* and *Update all* options update single linked elements or all publications files, respectively. The left-most column is the *Link* status indicator. The right-most column displays page number or other additional information. See Figures 25 and 26 for more details on these left and right outermost columns. Also see remaining figures for descriptions of the *Link info* and *Link options* buttons.

Figure 25. Link status indicator (left-hand column of Figure 24).

No indicator	Link is up to date or not linked
◆	Linked file has been modified and will automatically update
◇	Linked file has been modified and will not be automatically update
△	Both the linked file and the internal PageMaker file have been modified
(x)	Publication does not contain complete copy
?	Cannot find the external file

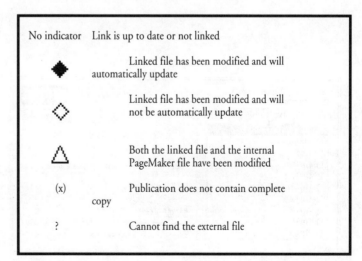

Page #	The linked inline graphic element is in a story that has not yet been composed; the page number is therefore unknown
LM	The left master page
RM	The right master page
PB	The pasteboard
OV	The linked text element - an inline graphic, for example, is not displayed because it is part of a text block that is overset, or not fully flowed
X	The linked text element is an open story that has not been placed

Figure 26. Right-hand column information of Figure 24 (other than page number).

Figure 27. The *Link info* dialog box can be accessed through the *Link info* button of Figure 24 or through the *Link info* command from the **Element** menu. The latter will apply only if a graphic or text block is selected.

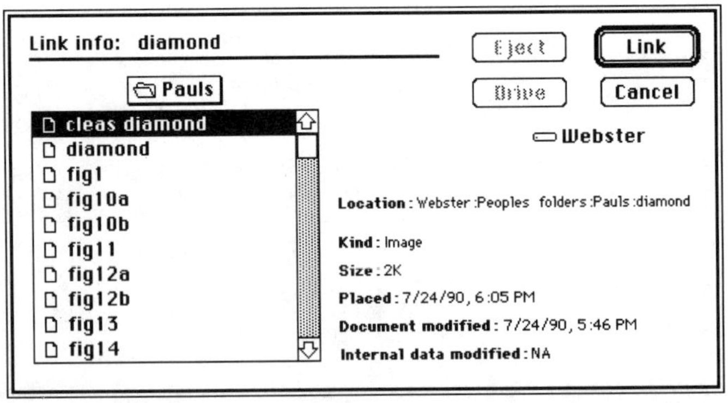

Figure 28. The *Link info* dialog box updates or re-establishes a link between text or graphic elements and the external file. This may be required if the external file is moved around or renamed.

Figure 29. The *Link options* dialog box can be accessed through the *Link options* button of Figure 24, or through the *Link options* command from the **Element** menu (if a linked element is selected).

Figure 30. The *Link options* dialog box. The three options that are available are designed to give control over how linked files are updated. These options are self-explanatory.

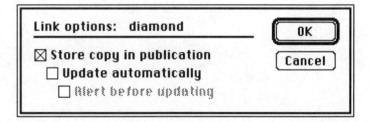

Figure 31. The *Link options: Defaults* dialog box is accessed by choosing the *Link options* command from the **Element** menu when no element is selected, or no publication is open. It can be used to set default values.

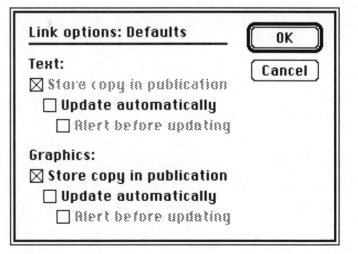

WORKING WITH TEXT

3

GENERAL EDITING

It is possible to edit text in PageMaker in normal layout view, or alternatively in story editor mode, which is the easier of the two methods of text editing. This latter mode is discussed in this chapter from Figure 65 through Figure 71. Here we look briefly at layout mode editing, as it is still useful for small text changes.

Text can be deleted and inserted in PageMaker in a similar fashion to a word processor. Insert the text tool cursor in the text and press the delete key for deletion to the left, or simply type in the text for insertion. When the flashing text cursor is inserted into text, it can be moved up, down, right or left by using the directional arrow keys on the keyboard. Alternatively, moving the mouse to a new location and clicking it, with the text tool selected, will result in a new text insertion point.

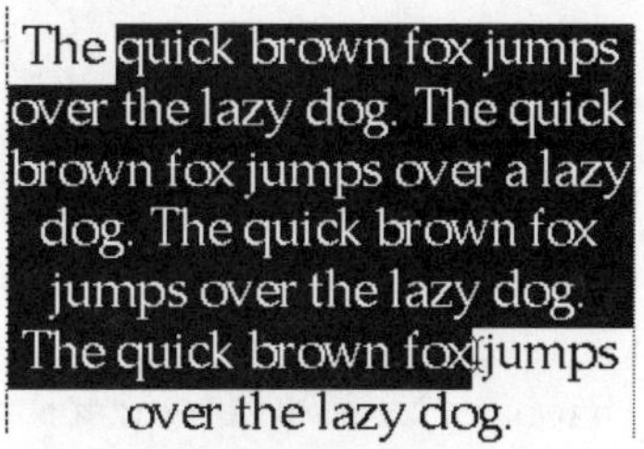

Figure 1. To copy or delete large blocks of text, the text needs to be highlighted first. This can be done in a number of ways. One way is to simply hold the mouse button down and move it over a section of text. Releasing the mouse button when required will select this text and highlight it in reverse video.

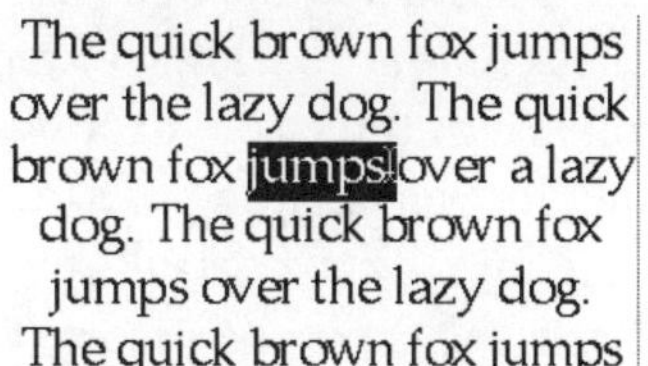

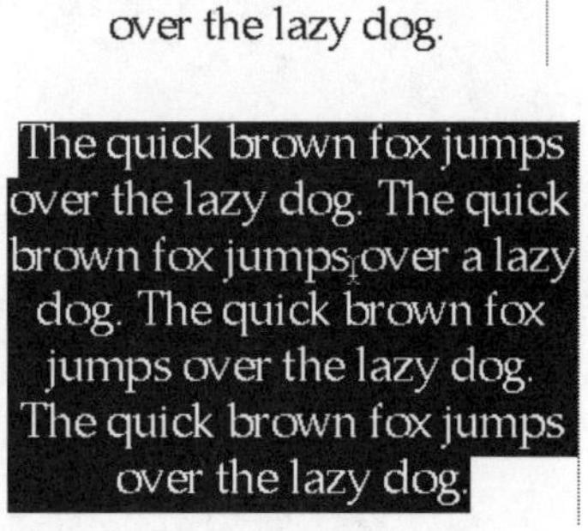

Figure 2. Double-clicking on a word will automatically select it. If you keep the mouse button held down after the double-click as you move through text, it will continue to highlight text a word at a time. The same procedure applies to paragraphs, but a triple-click is required initially.

The quick brown fox jumps over the lazy dog. The quick brown fox jumps over a lazy dog. The quick brown fox jumps over the lazy dog. The quick brown fox jumps over the lazy dog.

The quick brown fox jumps over the lazy dog. The quick brown fox jumps over a lazy dog. The quick brown fox jumps over the lazy dog. The quick brown fox jumps over the lazy dog.

The quick brown fox jumps over the lazy dog. The quick brown fox jumps over a lazy dog. The quick brown fox jumps over the lazy dog. The quick brown fox jumps over the lazy dog.

Figure 3. Two other methods of selection are possible for long stories. Insert the cursor anywhere in the text and choose *Select all* from the **Edit** menu. Alternatively, click the cursor once at the beginning of the text, move to the end of the text block, hold down the Shift key and click the mouse again. Everything in between these two points will be selected.

For the rest of the module, any reference to selecting or highlighting text, you may use any of the methods discussed in Figures 1 through 3.

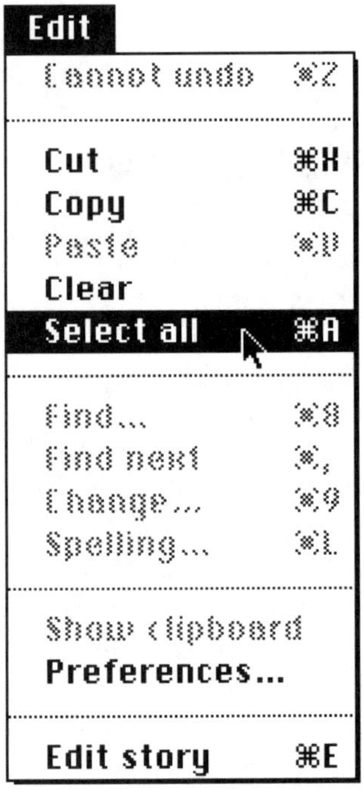

Edit	
Cannot undo	⌘Z
Cut	⌘H
Copy	⌘C
Paste	⌘D
Clear	
Select all	⌘A
Find...	⌘8
Find next	⌘,
Change...	⌘9
Spelling...	⌘L
Show clipboard	
Preferences...	
Edit story	⌘E

THE TYPE MENU

Figure 4. The **Type** menu is one of two menus within PageMaker 4 that has a series of sub-menus available. Each command with the ▶ symbol to the right will cause a sub-menu to appear. This sub-menu allows for rapid selection within a single command. If the commands within this menu are selected without first highlighting text (except for *Define styles*), you will be setting the text defaults for the publication. If text is first selected, then only the selected text is affected.

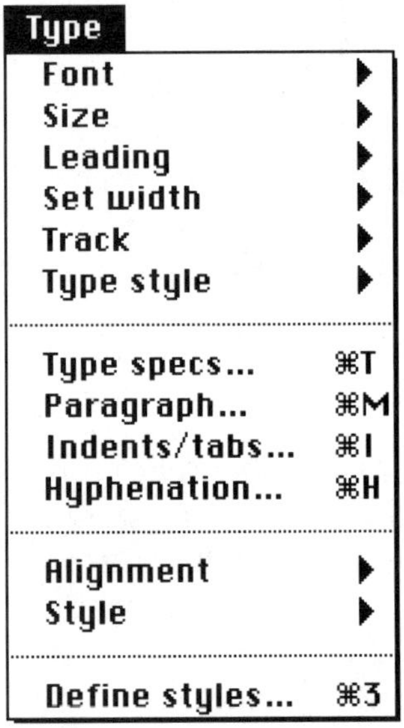

Type	
Font	▶
Size	▶
Leading	▶
Set width	▶
Track	▶
Type style	▶
Type specs...	⌘T
Paragraph...	⌘M
Indents/tabs...	⌘I
Hyphenation...	⌘H
Alignment	▶
Style	▶
Define styles...	⌘3

Figure 5. The *Font* command allows for selection of the different fonts on your computer. This may include all the PostScript printer fonts, and any additional downloadable fonts added to your system.

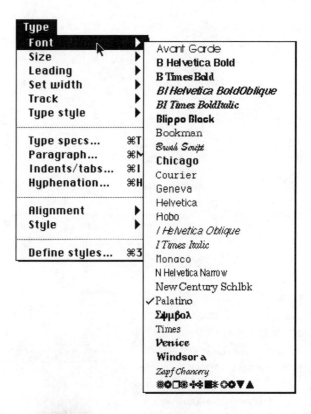

Figure 6. The *Size* command invokes a sub-menu as shown. Not all point sizes are available from within this sub-menu. Choosing *Other*, at the top, allows you to key in any font size between 4 and 650 points in 0.1 point increments.

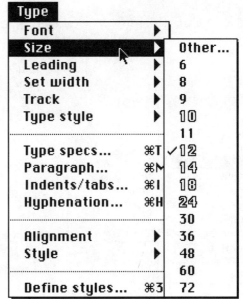

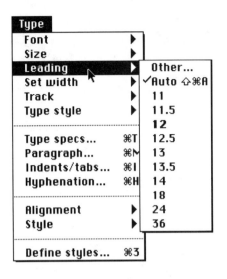

Figure 7. The sub-menu for the *Leading* command. You may choose any of the values shown or select *Other,* to key in your own value. *Other* allows you to choose a value from 0 to 1300 points in 0.1 point increments. *Auto,* by default, is set to 120% of the text point size. This percentage can be altered through the *Spacing* option in the *Paragraph specifications* dialog box (**Type** menu).

Figure 8. The *Set width* command controls the width of characters from 1% to 250% in 0.1% increments. Again, choose *Other* if you wish to have a specific value not included in the sub-menu as shown. This option allows you to condense or expand each individual letter character of any font.

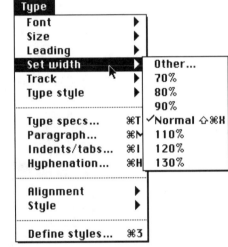

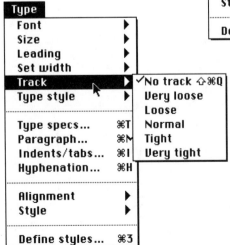

Figure 9. The *Track* command has its own sub-menu as shown. The purpose of this command is to adjust the spacing between characters. The only choices you have are the ones shown in this sub-menu.

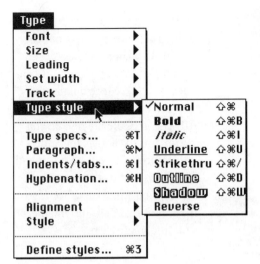

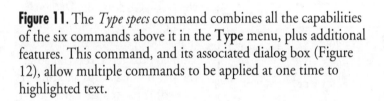

Figure 10. Simple style changes can be made to the text using the *Type style* command. The available options are shown in this sub-menu. All styles have to be applied one at a time, but multiple styles can be applied to the same piece of text.

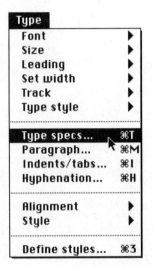

Figure 11. The *Type specs* command combines all the capabilities of the six commands above it in the **Type** menu, plus additional features. This command, and its associated dialog box (Figure 12), allow multiple commands to be applied at one time to highlighted text.

THE TYPE SPECIFICATIONS DIALOG BOX

Figure 12. The *Type specifications* dialog box. The *Font, Size, Leading, Set width*, and *Track* options provide similar drop down sub-menus as described above in Figures 5 through 9. The *Type style* selections at the bottom of the box are identical to those available in the *Type style* sub-menu of Figure 10. Additional capabilities in this dialog box are covered in Figures 13 and 14.

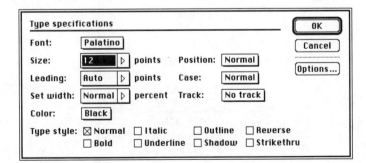

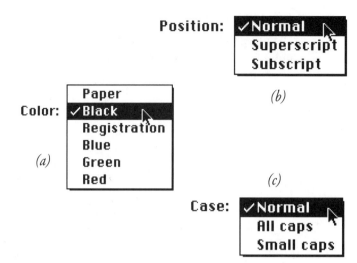

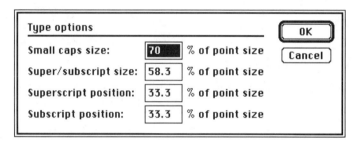

Figure 13. Three additional sub-menus are shown here from the Figure 12 dialog box. *Color* can be applied to text and graphics as shown in (a). More details on color may be found in Chapter 10, **Using Color**. The *Position* sub-menu (b) allows for Super/subscripting. The *Case* sub-menu (c) allows text to be converted to All caps or Small caps. See Figure 14 for more details on Small caps and Super/subscript.

Figure 14. Clicking on *Options* in the Figure 12 *Type specifications* dialog box provides the *Type Options* box. Here you can adjust the size of Small caps and Super/subscript, as well as Super/subscript positions.

THE PARAGRAPH SPECIFICATIONS DIALOG BOX

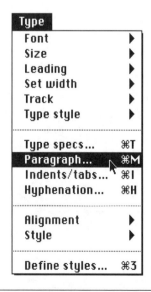

Figure 15. The *Paragraph* command and associated dialog box (Figure 16) include a range of options that will affect whole paragraphs, not individual text. These options are discussed in Figures 16 through 39.

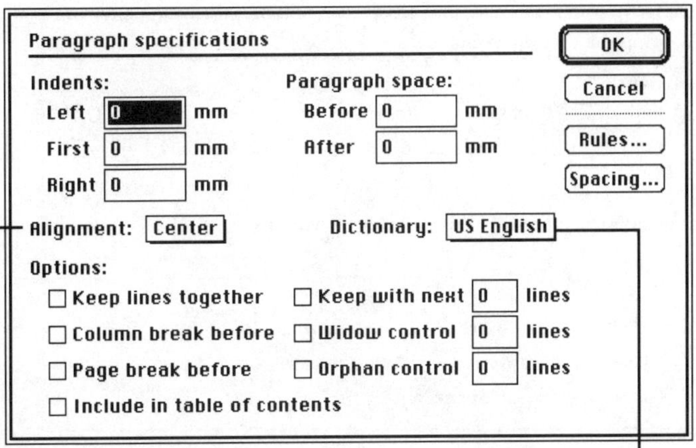

Figure 16. The *Paragraph specifications* dialog box. The five major options at the top include *Indents* (*Left* for the entire paragraph indent; *First* for first line only indent; and *Right* for entire paragraph right indent); and *Paragraph space.* (controls the amount of space *Before* and *After* your paragraph).

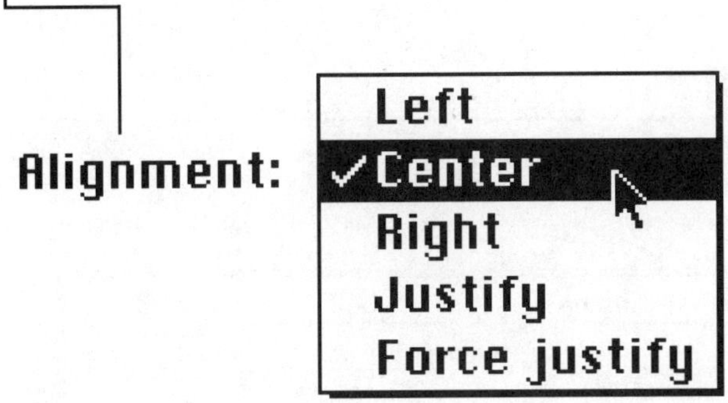

Paragraph specifications

Indents:	**Paragraph space:**
Left `0` mm	Before `0` mm
First `0` mm	After `0` mm
Right `0` mm	

OK
Cancel
Rules...
Spacing...

Alignment: `Center`   Dictionary: `US English`

Options:

☐ Keep lines together   ☐ Keep with next `0` lines
☐ Column break before   ☐ Widow control `0` lines
☐ Page break before   ☐ Orphan control `0` lines
☐ Include in table of contents

Figure 17. Holding the mouse down on the currently activated choice in the *Alignment* box, will reveal a sub-menu identical to the one that is available through the *Alignment* command toward the bottom of the **Type** menu.

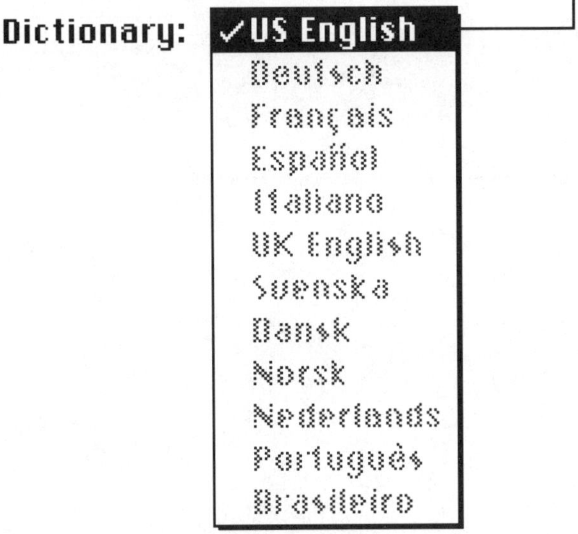

Alignment:

Left
✓Center
Right
Justify
Force justify

Figure 18. The *Dictionary* is used when checking spelling and hyphenation, and is activated by holding the mouse down on the currently displayed dictionary. Select your choice from the sub-menu that appears, if any others are available.

Dictionary:

✓US English
Deutsch
Français
Español
Italiano
UK English
Svenska
Dansk
Norsk
Nederlands
Português
Brasileiro

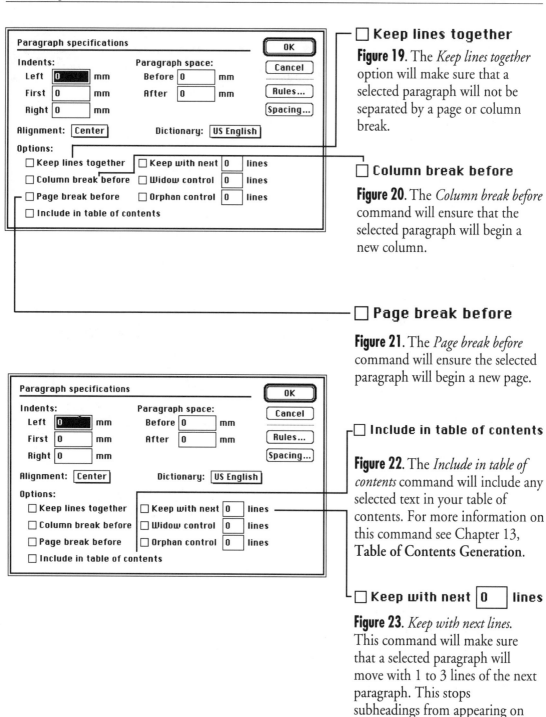

☐ Keep lines together

Figure 19. The *Keep lines together* option will make sure that a selected paragraph will not be separated by a page or column break.

☐ Column break before

Figure 20. The *Column break before* command will ensure that the selected paragraph will begin a new column.

☐ Page break before

Figure 21. The *Page break before* command will ensure the selected paragraph will begin a new page.

☐ Include in table of contents

Figure 22. The *Include in table of contents* command will include any selected text in your table of contents. For more information on this command see Chapter 13, **Table of Contents Generation.**

☐ Keep with next ⬚ lines

Figure 23. *Keep with next lines.* This command will make sure that a selected paragraph will move with 1 to 3 lines of the next paragraph. This stops subheadings from appearing on their own at the bottom of a column.

☐ **Widow control** [0] **lines**

Figure 24. To decide how many lines at the end of a paragraph will occur at the start of a new page or column, use the *Widow control* command. You have the option of leaving 1 to 3 lines here.

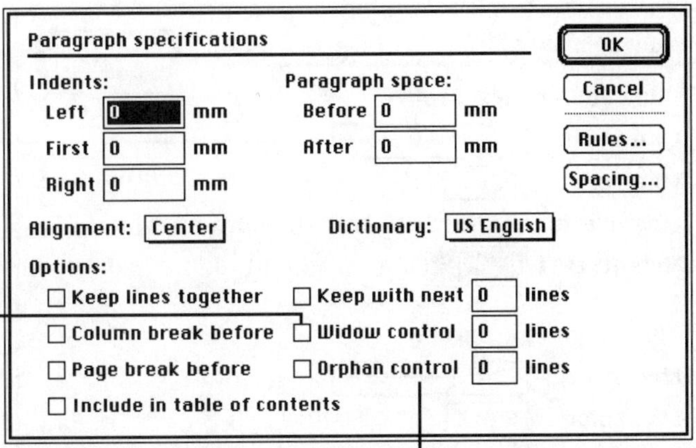

Paragraph specifications [OK]

Indents: Paragraph space: [Cancel]

Left [0] mm   Before [0] mm

First [0] mm   After [0] mm   [Rules...]

Right [0] mm   [Spacing...]

Alignment: [Center]   Dictionary: [US English]

Options:

☐ Keep lines together   ☐ Keep with next [0] lines

☐ Column break before   ☐ Widow control [0] lines

☐ Page break before   ☐ Orphan control [0] lines

☐ Include in table of contents

☐ **Orphan control** [0] **lines**

Figure 25. The *Orphan control* command works in a similar way to the *Widow control* command, only *Orphan control* decides how many lines at the start of a paragraph remain at the bottom of a column or page. The widow and orphan control options have to be preset when placing large documents.

PARAGRAPH RULES

Figure 26. This dialog box will appear after you click on *Rules* in the *Paragraph specifications* dialog box of Figure 16. This dialog box lets you place lines above and below your text. You are able to set the above and below rules separately, and you may have one without the other. These rules are activated by clicking inside the *Rule above paragraph* and/or the *Rule below paragraph* selection box(es).

See Figures 27 through 32 on how to set the various *Paragraph rules* options.

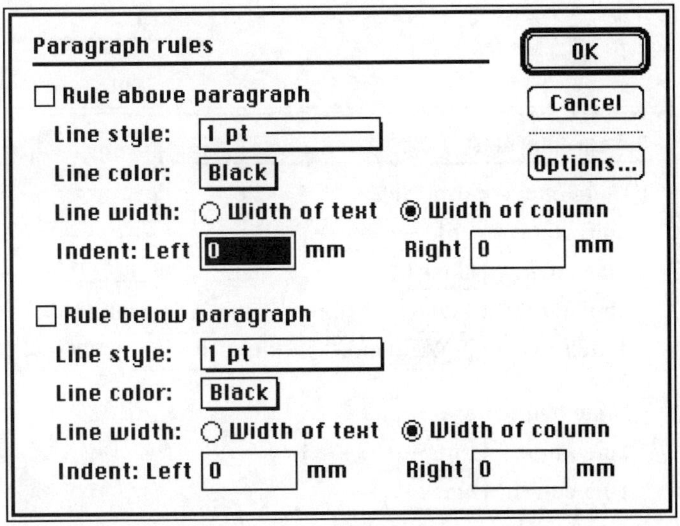

Paragraph rules [OK]

☐ **Rule above paragraph**   [Cancel]

Line style: [1 pt ———]

Line color: [Black]   [Options...]

Line width: ○ **Width of text**   ● **Width of column**

Indent: Left [0] mm   Right [0] mm

☐ **Rule below paragraph**

Line style: [1 pt ———]

Line color: [Black]

Line width: ○ **Width of text**   ● **Width of column**

Indent: Left [0] mm   Right [0] mm

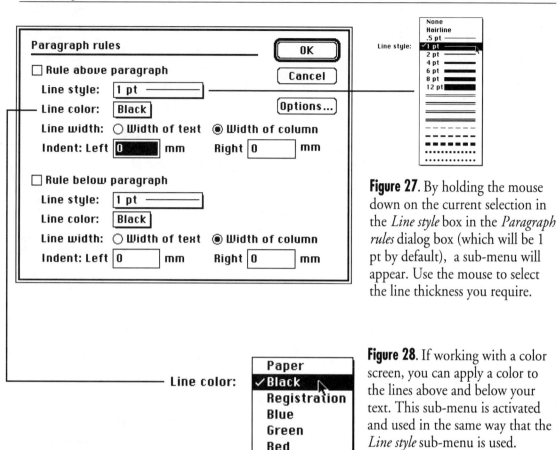

Figure 27. By holding the mouse down on the current selection in the *Line style* box in the *Paragraph rules* dialog box (which will be 1 pt by default), a sub-menu will appear. Use the mouse to select the line thickness you require.

Figure 28. If working with a color screen, you can apply a color to the lines above and below your text. This sub-menu is activated and used in the same way that the *Line style* sub-menu is used.

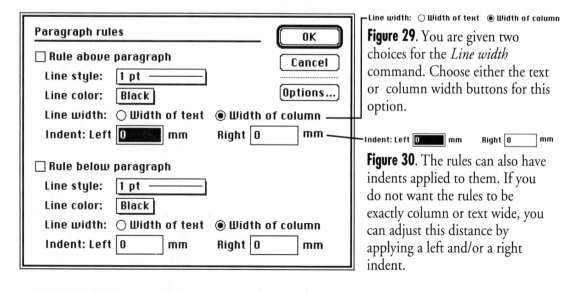

Figure 29. You are given two choices for the *Line width* command. Choose either the text or column width buttons for this option.

Figure 30. The rules can also have indents applied to them. If you do not want the rules to be exactly column or text wide, you can adjust this distance by applying a left and/or a right indent.

Figure 31. The options for the *Rule below paragraph* are exactly the same as are the options for the *Rule above paragraph*.

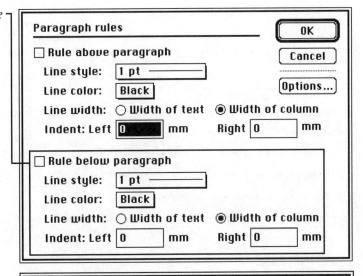

PARAGRAPH RULE OPTIONS

Figure 32. The *Paragraph rule options* dialog box is activated by clicking on the *Options* command in the *Paragraph rules* dialog box (Figure 31). The *Top* and *Bottom* options allow you to alter the distance that the Rules sit above and below the text. Double-click in the relevant box and type in the new value to give the ruling lines more space between themselves and the text.

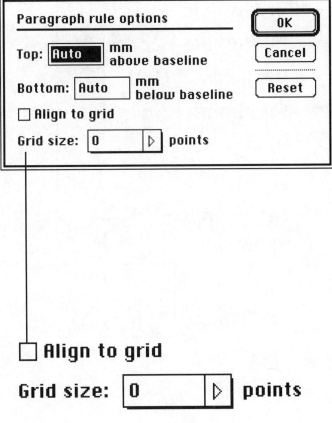

Figure 33. The *Align to grid* command ensures that the body text on your page will align horizontally. When using this command, the *Grid size* option should reflect the setting you have for the body text's leading.

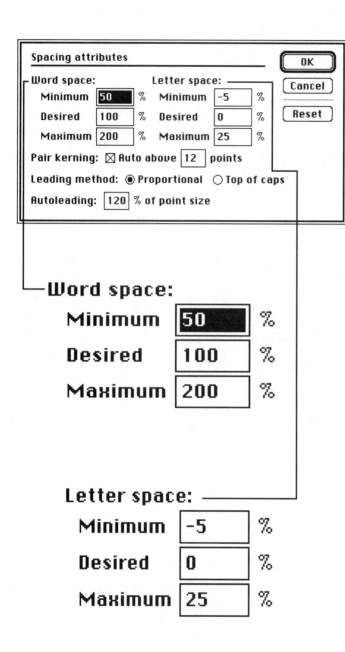

SPACING ATTRIBUTES

Figure 34. The *Spacing attributes* dialog box is activated by clicking on the *Spacing* option in the *Paragraph specifications* dialog box of Figure 16.

Figure 35. *Word space.* This command will affect the spacing between your words. The settings for each option can range from 0% to 500%. Increasing or decreasing these figures will increase or decrease the word spacing respectively.

Figure 36. The *Letter space* option only works with justified text. The range available for *Minimum* and *Maximum* is -200% to +200%. The desired figure should be between the minimum and maximum settings. Again, increasing and decreasing the settings here will be reflected in the selected text.

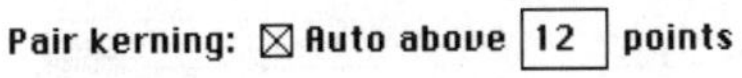

Pair kerning: ⊠ **Auto above** [12] **points**

Figure 37. The *Pair kerning* option varies the amount of space between sets of characters. By default, *Auto above* will be selected.

Leading method: ◉ **Proportional** ○ **Top of caps**

Figure 38. The *Leading method* selection should nearly always be *Proportional*. The *Top of caps* method is useful for special design effects.

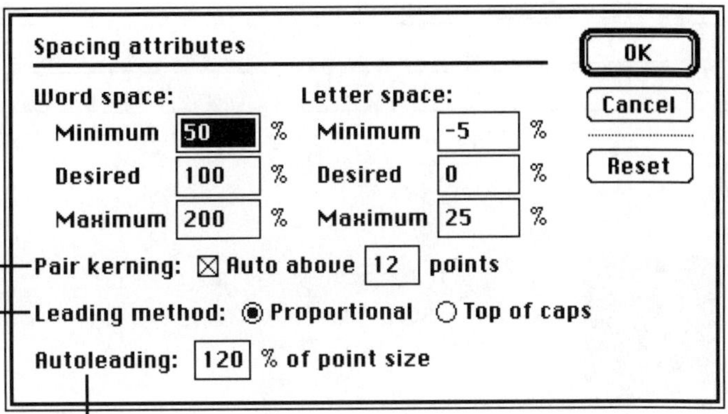

Spacing attributes

Word space:

Minimum	50	%
Desired	100	%
Maximum	200	%

Letter space:

Minimum	-5	%
Desired	0	%
Maximum	25	%

OK

Cancel

Reset

Pair kerning: ⊠ Auto above [12] points

Leading method: ◉ Proportional ○ Top of caps

Autoleading: [120] % of point size

Autoleading: [120] % of point size

Figure 39. The *Autoleading* is set to 120% by default. This figure represents a proportion of the point size, and changing this figure will affect the line spacing of the text.

INDENTS/TABS COMMAND

Figure 40. The *Indents/tabs* command which leads to the dialog box of Figure 41.

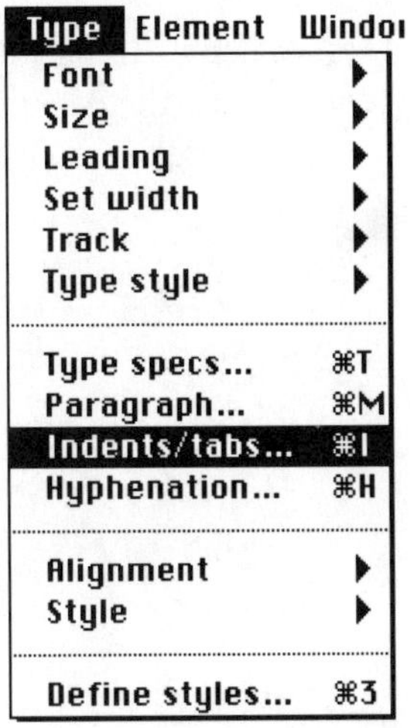

Type Element Windo⟩

Font	▶
Size	▶
Leading	▶
Set width	▶
Track	▶
Type style	▶
Type specs...	⌘T
Paragraph...	⌘M
Indents/tabs...	⌘I
Hyphenation...	⌘H
Alignment	▶
Style	▶
Define styles...	⌘3

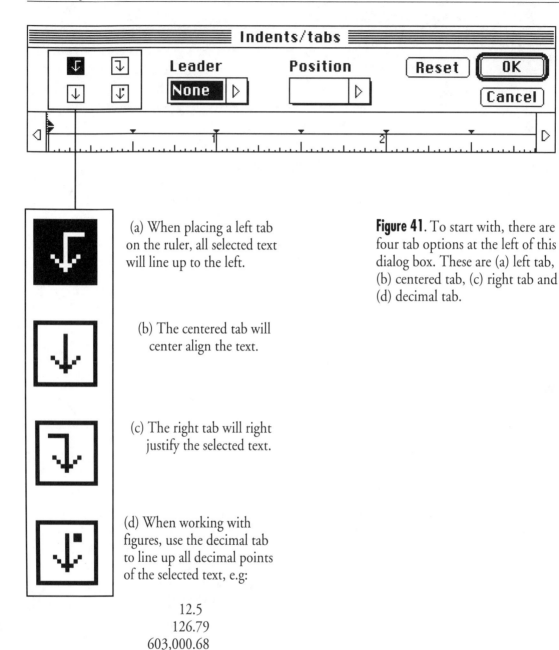

(a) When placing a left tab on the ruler, all selected text will line up to the left.

(b) The centered tab will center align the text.

(c) The right tab will right justify the selected text.

(d) When working with figures, use the decimal tab to line up all decimal points of the selected text, e.g:

12.5
126.79
603,000.68

Figure 41. To start with, there are four tab options at the left of this dialog box. These are (a) left tab, (b) centered tab, (c) right tab and (d) decimal tab.

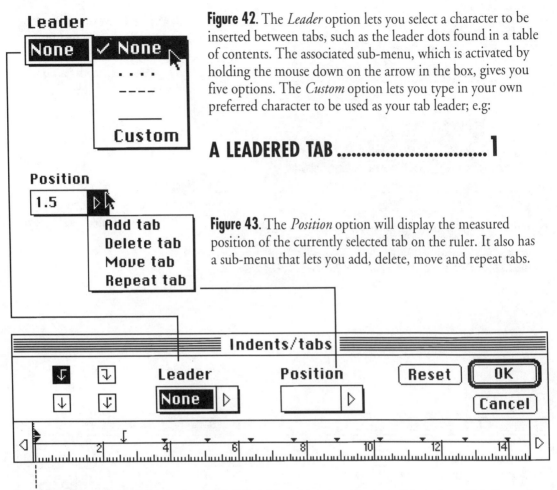

Figure 42. The *Leader* option lets you select a character to be inserted between tabs, such as the leader dots found in a table of contents. The associated sub-menu, which is activated by holding the mouse down on the arrow in the box, gives you five options. The *Custom* option lets you type in your own preferred character to be used as your tab leader; e.g:

A LEADERED TAB 1

Figure 43. The *Position* option will display the measured position of the currently selected tab on the ruler. It also has a sub-menu that lets you add, delete, move and repeat tabs.

Figure 44. On activating the *Indents/tabs* dialog box, the 0 (zero) point of the ruler will indicate the beginning of the selected text. This dialog box can be moved around the page by holding the mouse down on the top striped bar and dragging it to a new position.

Figure 45. The ruler has two markers that start at the zero position but can be altered by you. The top marker represents the first line indent of the selected paragraph. Moving this marker with the mouse will alter the position of the first line of your selected text.

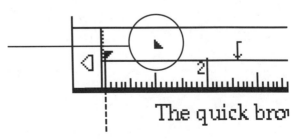

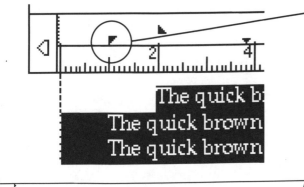

Figure 46. The bottom marker is the left indent of the whole paragraph, and all selected text will move to reflect the amount the marker is moved by the mouse.

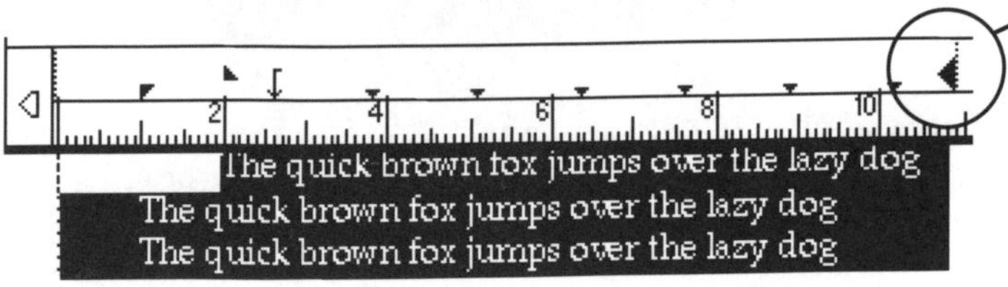

Figure 47. The right indent marker sits on the ruler at the right margin of the selected text.

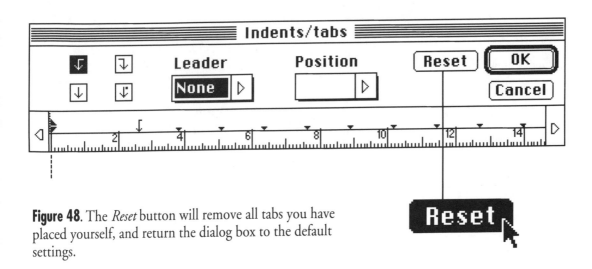

Figure 48. The *Reset* button will remove all tabs you have placed yourself, and return the dialog box to the default settings.

HYPHENATION

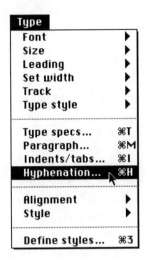

Figure 49. The next command in the **Type** menu is the *Hyphenation* command.

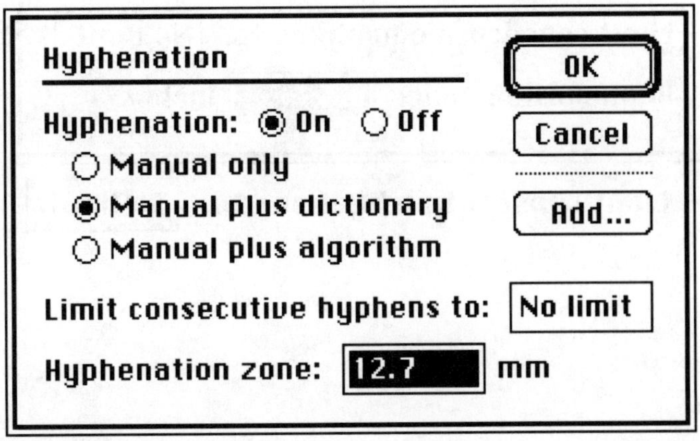

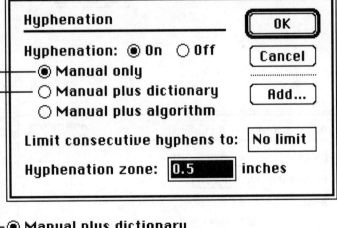

Figure 50. The *Hyphenation* dialog box. By default the hyphenation will be on.

Figure 51. The *Manual only* choice in this dialog box will only hyphenate where you have placed discretionary hyphens (Command + hyphen). These discretionary hyphens will only appear when a word that has one of these hyphens falls at the end of a line. It will be split to fit the paragraph correctly.

Figure 52. The *Manual plus dictionary* choice will be selected by default. All discretionary hyphens, plus the hyphens that appear in PageMaker's dictionary, will be used when this option is selected.

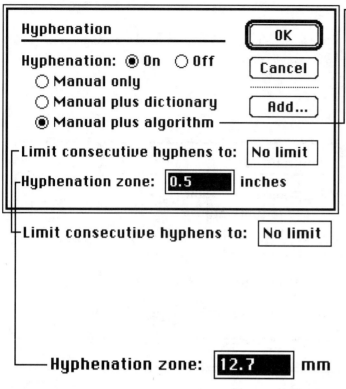

Figure 53. The *Manual plus algorithm* option will hyphenate any word whether it appears in the PageMaker dictionary or not. If a word lands at the end of a column, PageMaker will hyphenate this word where it calculates the most suitable place.

Figure 54. The *Limit consecutive hyphens to* option lets you set a maximum number of consecutive hyphens you would like to appear (from 1 to 255) in the selected text.

Figure 55. The *Hyphenation zone* option affects the amount of space used before hyphenation occurs. The larger the figure you place in this box, the less the number of hyphens that will occur.

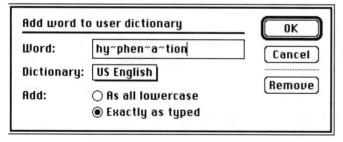

Figure 56. Clicking on the *Add* option in the *Hyphenation* dialog box of Figure 50 will activate this dialog box. Here you can add words to your dictionary and select your preferred place of hyphenation. It is also possible to change the position of hyphens in words that already exist in the dictionary. Placing one hyphen in a word indicates that this is the first place you would like the word to be split. Two hyphens represents your second choice, and three indicates your last choice. Create hyphenation points using a tilde (~).

Figure 57. The *Alignment* command, and its associated sub-menu, has the same alignment choices available as through the *Paragraph specifications* command.

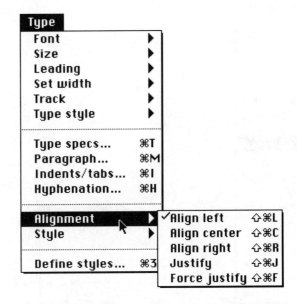

Figure 58. The *Style* and *Define styles* commands are explained in Chapter 9 — **Using Style Sheets**.

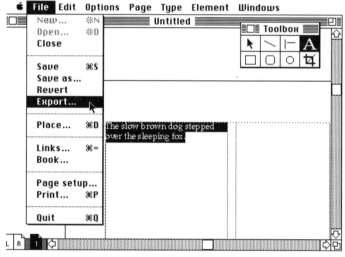

EXPORTING TEXT

Figure 59. Through the *Export* command in the **File** menu, text created in PageMaker (or imported text) can be exported to an outside word processing program.

Figure 60. Before choosing the *Export* command, select the text that you would like to export. The amount of text is not important

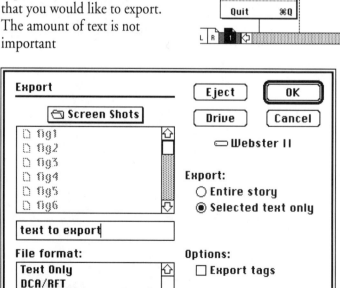

Figure 61. The *Export* dialog box. Here you give the file a name. You can also select the drive or folder where you would like to save this file.

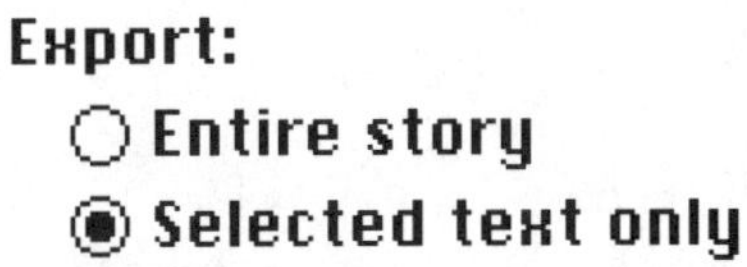

Export:
  ○ **Entire story**
  ◉ **Selected text only**

Figure 62. You also have the option of exporting the entire story or just the selected text.

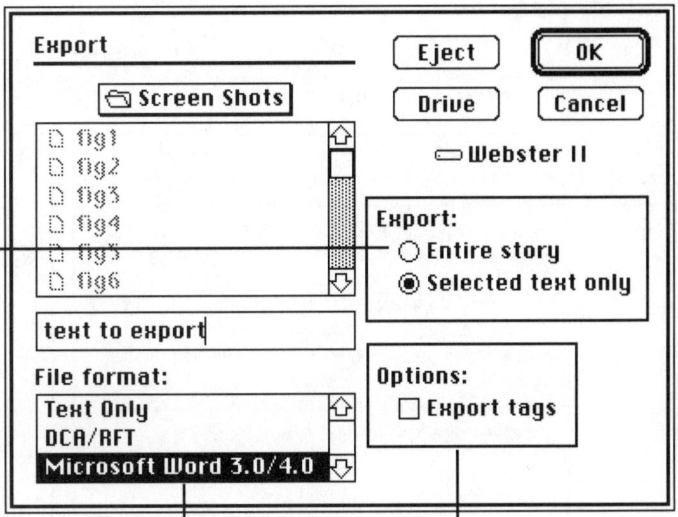

```
┌─────────────────────────────────────────────────────────────┐
│  Export _____        [ Eject ]    [   OK   ]       │
│         [ 🗁 Screen Shots ]      [ Drive ]   [ Cancel ]       │
│   🗋 fig1                ⇧           ⊂⊃ Webster II            │
│   🗋 fig2                                                      │
│   🗋 fig3              ░░░         ┌──────────────────────┐   │
│   🗋 fig4              ░░░         │ Export:              │   │
│   🗋 fig5              ░░░         │  ○ Entire story      │   │
│   🗋 fig6                ⇩         │  ◉ Selected text only│   │
│                                    └──────────────────────┘   │
│  [ text to export|            ]                               │
│  File format:                    ┌──────────────────────┐    │
│  ┌──────────────────────┐ ⇧      │ Options:             │    │
│  │ Text Only            │        │  ☐ Export tags       │    │
│  │ DCA/RFT              │        └──────────────────────┘    │
│  │ Microsoft Word 3.0/4.0│ ⇩                                 │
│  └──────────────────────┘                                     │
└─────────────────────────────────────────────────────────────┘
```

Options:
  ☐ **Export tags**

Figure 63. The *Export tags* option is selected if you want the styles created for your text in PageMaker to be exported as well.

Figure 64. *File format* lets you select the format in which you would like to export the file. Scrolling down the list of options available using the arrows to the right of the box, will allow you to find and select the appropriate file format. After you have set up the *Export* dialog box in the desired way, click on OK.

File format:

```
┌──────────────────────────┐
│ Text Only             ⇧  │
│ DCA/RFT                  │
│ Microsoft Word 3.0/4.0 ⇩ │
└──────────────────────────┘
```

STORY EDITOR

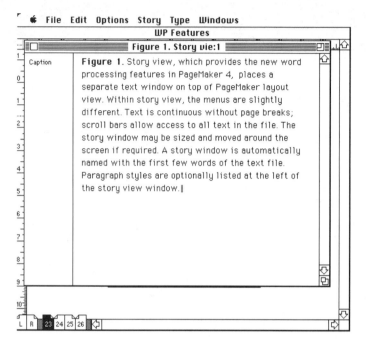

Figure 65. Story view, which provides the new word processing features in PageMaker 4, places a separate text window on top of PageMaker layout view. Within story view, the menus are slightly different. Text is continuous without page breaks; scroll bars allow access to all text in the file. The story window may be sized and moved around the screen if required. A story window is automatically named with the first few words of the text file. Paragraph styles are optionally listed at the left of the story view window.

Figure 66. Story view is accessed in a variety of ways. Inserting the text cursor in a story and choosing *Edit story* from the **Edit** menu is one way; another way is to move between story editor view and publication layout using the **Windows** menu. It is also possible to triple-click with the pointer tool on text to move automatically into story view. Clicking on an exposed part of an open story window will also move you into story view. If you have no text on the page you may select the *Edit story* command, and the story window will appear ready for you to key text in as a new story.

Figure 67. Returning to layout view from story view is achieved in a number of ways. Clicking the close box in the story window will achieve this requirement, as will choosing the *Close story* command from the **Story** menu. Choosing *Edit layout* from **Edit** menu, or clicking on an exposed portion of the layout view publication, are two other methods which can be used. If you have not yet placed your story (e.g. if you activated story editor to type in a text file), PageMaker will give you the option of placing this text or discarding it.

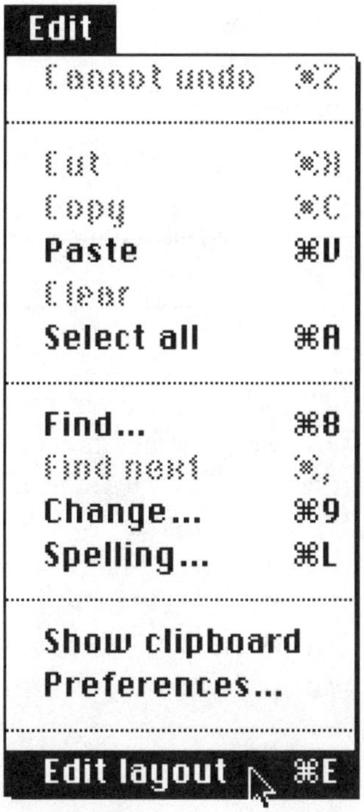

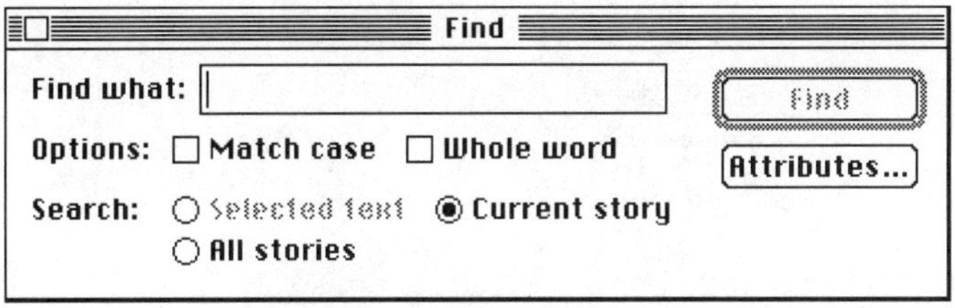

Figure 68. The *Find* command, from the **Edit** menu in story view, allows you to search for text and other attributes while in story view. The associated dialog box allows you to insert the text to be found. The search may occur over selected text, the current story, or all stories.

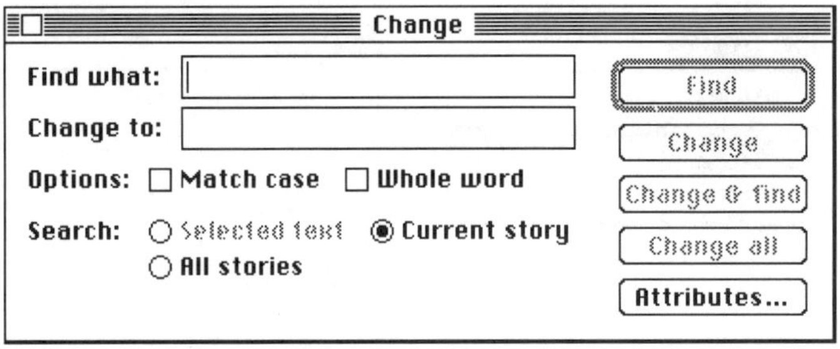

Figure 69. The *Change* command from the **Edit** menu in story view searches for, and replaces, selected text with new text. The *Find what:* and *Change to:* lines of this dialog box are self-explanatory. You have a number of choices throughout this process which include *Find, Change, Change & find* or *Change all.* Note, in the bottom right of the dialog box you can also choose to search for attributes, as well as text (i.e., style attributes applied to text).

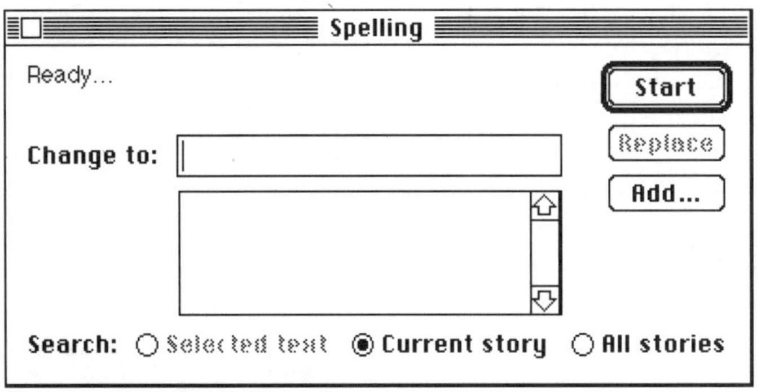

Figure 70. Spell checking is possible by choosing the *Spelling* command from the **Edit** menu while in story view. Click on *Start* to commence the spell check. As a misspelled word is detected, it is displayed in the dialog box, as well as possible alternatives in the bottom rectangle. You may select a PageMaker suggestion, or key in your own correct spelling.

Figure 71. The *Import* command from the **Story** menu allows text and graphics to be imported into the story window. The *Import to Story Editor* dialog box allows you to choose the file you wish to import.

Graphics will not appear as graphics in story view, but will be seen as small markers. You also have the option of importing graphics as inline or independent. See Chapter 6 for more information on inline and independent graphics.

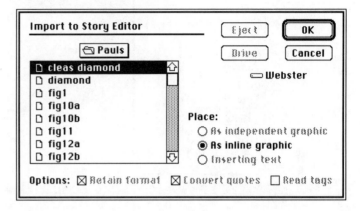

MANIPULATING TEXT BLOCKS

MOVING TEXT BLOCKS

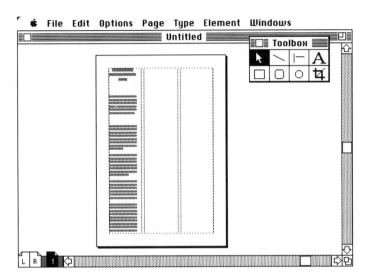

Figure 72. When PageMaker loads text onto a page (or pages), it does so in what are called text blocks. These text blocks can be manipulated using the pointer tool in a variety of ways. This figure shows text loaded into one column of a three column page. We will now look at different ways to manipulate this text block.

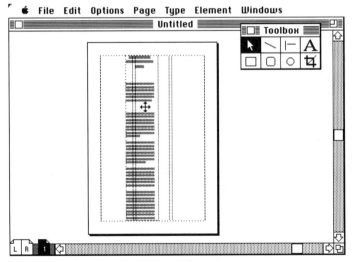

Figure 73. Using the pointer tool (note pointer tool selected in the toolbox), you can hold the mouse down on the text block and move it anywhere on the page. In this figure, we have held the mouse down on the block for a few seconds, and then moved the mouse to the right. This results in the text block moving as shown. If we had held our mouse down on the block and moved it quickly, only a boxed outline of the text would move. The end result, however, is the same — the text block is moved to a new location.

RESIZING TEXT BLOCKS

Figure 74. As well as being repositioned, text blocks can be adjusted in size horizontally, vertically and/or diagonally. The various handles of a selected text block that are required for resizing, are shown in this figure.

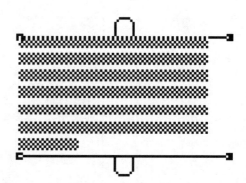

Figure 75. The corner squares of the text block allow you to resize a block in any direction. You simply grab the corner handle with the mouse pointer tool, and move it in any direction you like. The text block can be resized horizontally, vertically and diagonally using this method. If the text block is enlarged, additional text (assuming more text is available) will appear.

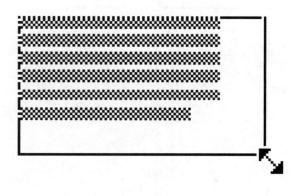

Figure 76. If a text block has a windowshade handle that has a ▼ symbol in it, then more text is available to flow onto the page. Grabbing this handle with the pointer tool and pulling it downwards, resizes the block vertically, and will show any additional text that belongs to this particular text block.

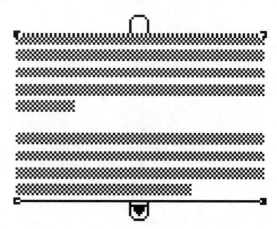

ADJUSTING TEXT BLOCKS

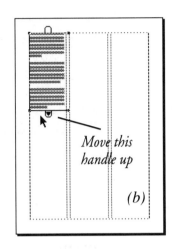

(a)

(b)

Move this handle up

Figure 77. Here we have a text block that has flowed down column one (a). No further text is contained in this story. We now wish to break this text block into three parts and place it in columns 2 and 3 as well. Select the block with the pointer tool and move the bottom windowshade handle up to approximately one-third down the column (b). Now see Figure 78.

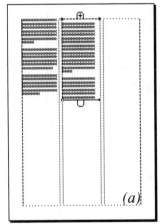

(a)

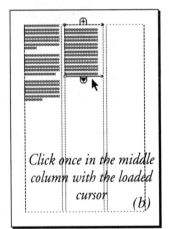

Click once in the middle column with the loaded cursor

(b)

Figure 78. Click once on the bottom windowshade handle in Figure 77(b), and place the loaded text cursor at the top of the middle column. Click here as we have done in (a), to flow the text down this column. Now grab the bottom windowshade handle and pull it up to approximately one third again as shown in (b). Now see Figure 79.

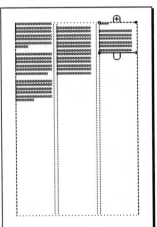

Figure 79. Click once on the bottom windowshade handle from Figure 78(b) and place the loaded text cursor at the top of column three. Click here as we have done to flow text down this column. We have now broken the text into three separate blocks.

CAN YOU LOSE TEXT?

PageMaker can manipulate text blocks in a variety of ways. For example, the middle text block of Figure 79 can be removed by simply grabbing the bottom windowshade handle and pulling it right up to the top. Then click anywhere on the page to remove this block without losing text. The text from the middle block will now flow into column three. The size of column three will not immediately change, but will now have a down arrow symbol indicating that more text is available to be placed on the page.

So far, we have been describing text blocks which are all part of the same story. It is sometimes necessary to take a text block and make it an independent, separate text block from the original text file or story. This is called *unthreading* text. The reverse process — *threading* text — is when you join an independent text block, which is not part of the original story, to become united with this text file.

Figures 80 through 82 show how to unthread text. Figures 83 through 86 show how to thread text.

UNTHREADING TEXT

Figure 80. Let's say you wish to unthread the middle column text block of this figure. Select this text block with the pointer tool and choose *Cut* from the **Edit** menu.

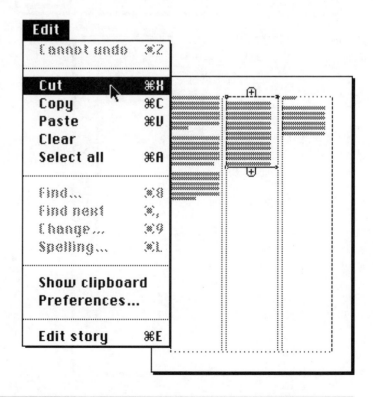

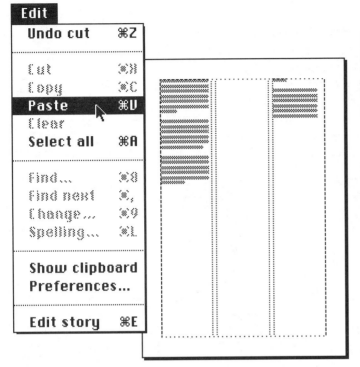

Figure 81. The selected text block has disappeared from the screen. To bring it back, but not as part of the same story, select *Paste* from the **Edit** menu.

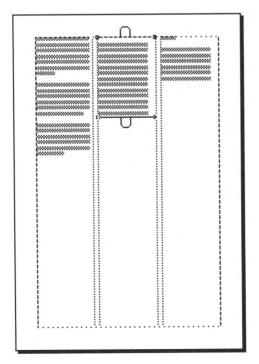

Figure 82. The text block has returned to the middle column. However, this text block is not part of the original story. It can be changed, edited, modified etc., without affecting the other two columns. This is indicated by the empty windowshade handles at both the top and bottom of this middle text block.

THREADING TEXT

Figure 83. To rethread the text block of Figure 82 back into the original story, select this block with the pointer tool, and choose the *Cut* command from the **Edit** menu.

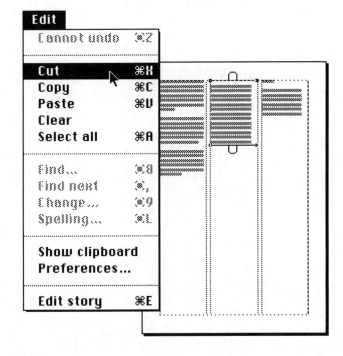

Figure 84. The text block is now removed from the page. Next, select the text tool and insert it within the text, wherever you wish the deleted text block to reappear.

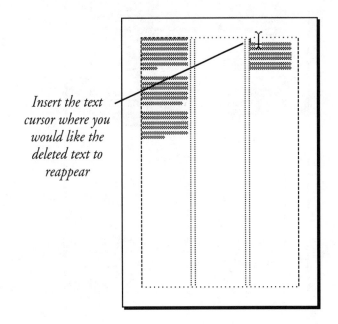

Insert the text cursor where you would like the deleted text to reappear

Figure 85. Now choose the *Paste* command from the **Edit** menu.

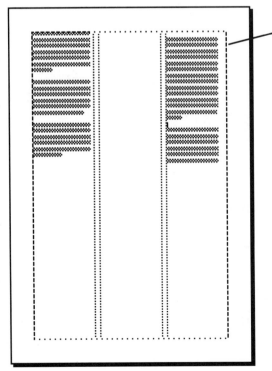

Figure 86. The text has flowed back onto the page to become part of the original story again.

ROTATING TEXT

Figure 87. Text can be rotated within PageMaker at 90 degree intervals. Select the text block with the pointer tool, then choose the *Text rotation* command from the **Element** menu.

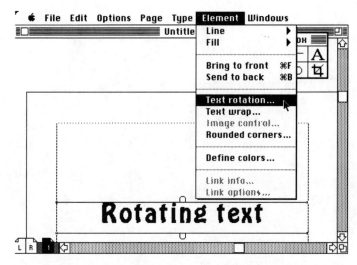

Figure 88. The *Text rotation* dialog box shows the choices available. We have chosen the second choice from the left. The result is shown in Figure 89.

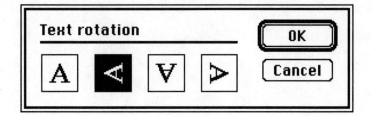

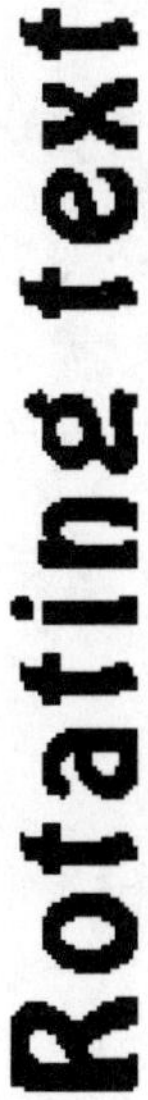

Figure 89. The result of rotating the text to -90 degrees. Note that longer text blocks can also be rotated in this fashion.

MASTER PAGES

MASTER PAGE CONCEPT

Every PageMaker document has a master page. The master page stores information that you wish to appear on every page of a document. Whether the document is double-sided or single-sided (which in turn affects the master page setup) is determined in the *Page setup* dialog box.

Figure 1. The master pages are denoted by an L and R icon to the left of the normal page number icons. If PageMaker is set up as a single-sided document, only the R icon will be present.

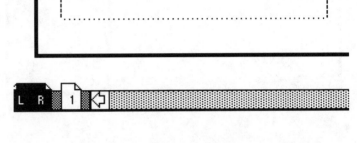

Figure 2. Here we are displaying the left and right master pages. These pages are identical in operation to all other PageMaker pages, except for some important considerations. First, you cannot directly print the contents of the master pages. Second, anything (text or graphics) that is included on the master pages will normally repeat on all other pages in your publication. This is useful if you have a company logo, headers, footers, etc., that you wish to include on every page in your document.

Simply put them on the left or right master page and they will, unless turned off, appear on every left or right page in your publication.

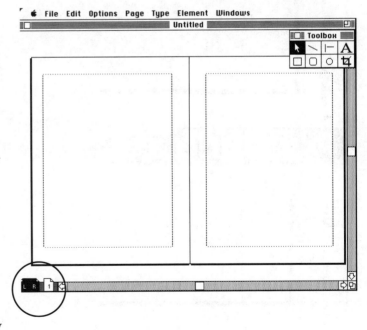

AUTOMATIC PAGE NUMBERING

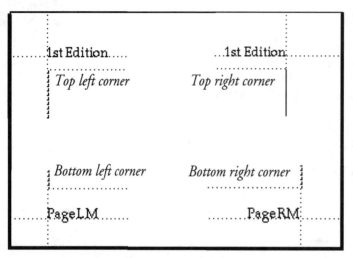

Figure 3. Here we have enlarged the four corners of the left and right master pages. The top left and right corners have included a header each, and the bottom left and right corners include a page number as a footer. The page number is inserted on the master pages by keying Command + Option + P with the text tool, at the required locations. The page number, appearing as LM and RM on the left and right master pages, automatically updates to reflect the correct number on every page. The headers, like the page number, will also appear on every page.

Figure 4. It is also possible to place fixed wording on the master page in front of the page number. This fixed wording, in our case 3 (for denoting part of Chapter 3), will now appear on every page as part of the page numbering system.

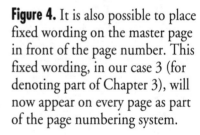

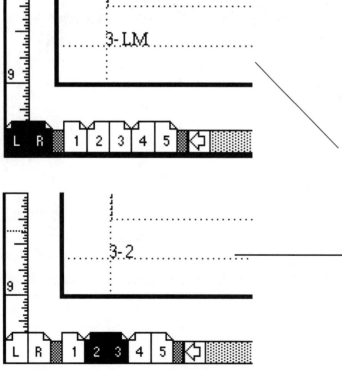

(a) The fixed character (3) is placed on the master page, denoting the whole publication is part of Chapter 3.

(b) Page 2 of the publication reflects the numbering format of 3-2, being page 2 of Chapter 3.

Figure 5. The page number that appears on a page is the same as the icon that appears in the bottom left-hand corner of the screen. The actual page number can be altered, as shown here, by adjusting the *Start page #* box in the *Page setup* dialog box from the File menu.

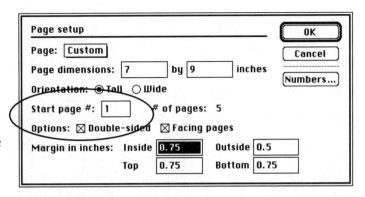

Figure 6. The *Page numbering* box, obtained through clicking on the *Numbers* button in the Figure 5 *Page setup* dialog box, allows a choice of numbering system to be utilized. You may choose from the different options shown in this dialog box.

GUIDES ON MASTER PAGES

Figure 7. Apart from headers, footers and page numbers, the master pages are used to set up column guides, ruler guides and other constant elements, such as a company logo. Here we have set up, through the *Column guides* command, three columns on both the left and right master pages, two vertical and two horizontal ruler guides, two headers, two footers and a logo. These will now appear on all pages of the publication (unless turned off on a per page basis). See Figure 8 for the results of these master page items on pages 2 and 3 of the document.

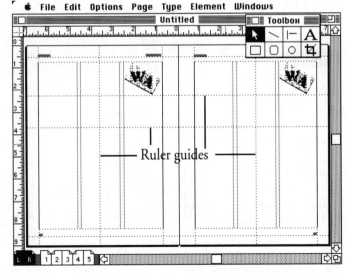

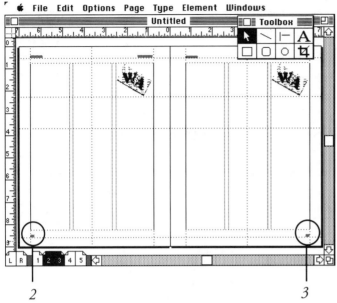

Figure 8. We are now displaying pages 2 and 3. All items from the master pages are now showing, exactly as they appear on the master pages of Figure 7.

See Figures 9 through 11 on how to remove master page items from selected pages.

REMOVING MASTER PAGE ITEMS

Figure 9. Text or graphics, created on the master page, cannot be selected in the normal way by the pointer tool, and deleted from a particular page. You can only select and manipulate master page text or graphics on the master pages. To delete all master page items from the currently active page or pages, select the *Display master items* command from the **Page** menu. All master page items will then disappear from the screen as shown here.

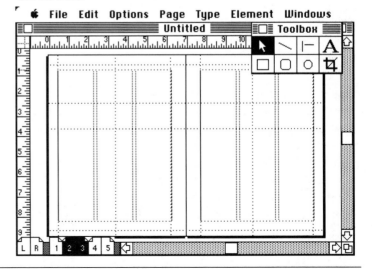

Figure 10. If you only wish to delete certain master page items on a particular page, simply draw a white box over them. In this case, we have drawn a white box over the top left header to hide it from printing on page one. This can be done for any number of master page items you wish to hide. (A white box is denoted by a *Paper Fill* and *Line None* from the **Element** menu.)

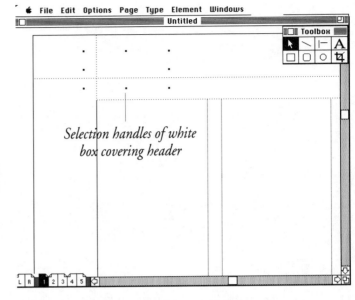

Selection handles of white box covering header

Figure 11. Column, ruler, or margin guides can be adjusted on any page, even though they may have been created on the master pages. Here we have adjusted the column and ruler guides, compared to how they were in Figure 8. If we wish to revert back to the original non-printing guides as for Figure 8, we would choose the *Copy master guides* command from the **Page** menu.

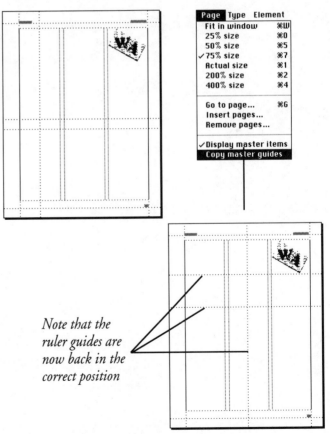

Note that the ruler guides are now back in the correct position

PageMaker Graphics

The Drawing Tools

PageMaker's graphic tools, contained in the toolbox, allow for a variety of graphic objects to be drawn within PageMaker.

Figure 1. The Toolbox contains the several drawing tools required to create internal graphics.

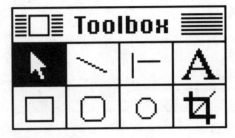

The diagonal line drawing tool for drawing lines at any angle.

The perpendicular line drawing tool for drawing lines at 45 degree increments.

The square-corner drawing tool for drawing rectangles and squares.

The rounded-corner drawing tool for drawing rectangles and squares.

The oval drawing tool for drawing ellipses and circles.

Drawing Graphics

Figure 2. To draw a graphic, select the appropriate tool, hold down the mouse, and drag it across the page. You can drag in any direction.

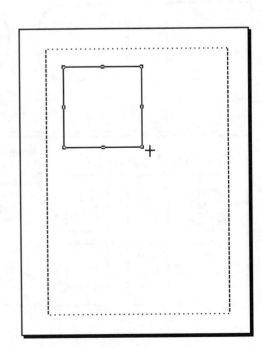

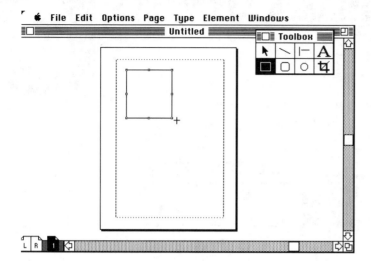

Figure 3. Release the mouse when finished. The graphic is then selected. (Note the eight small square dots or handles around the edge of the graphic.)

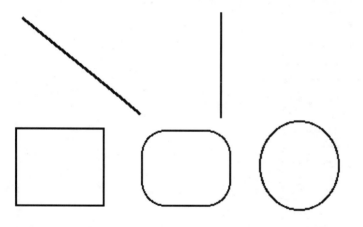

Figure 4. Examples of different graphics.

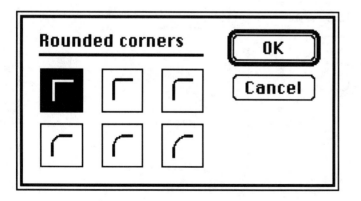

Figure 5. The *Rounded corners* dialog box allows various radius options to be chosen, when drawing rectangles or squares, with the rounded-corner drawing tool.

Figure 6. Graphics are automatically selected after you have drawn them. They will become deselected once you choose another tool from the toolbox. To re-select a graphic, click on its edge with the pointer tool, or draw a square around the graphic with your finger on the mouse and the pointer tool selected.

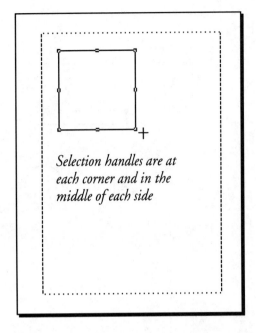

Selection handles are at each corner and in the middle of each side

Figure 7. Multiple graphics can be selected in any one of the following ways:

(a) By selecting each graphic with the Shift key depressed.

(b) By drawing an imaginary box around all graphics with the pointer tool.

(c) Choosing the *Select all* command from the **Edit** menu.

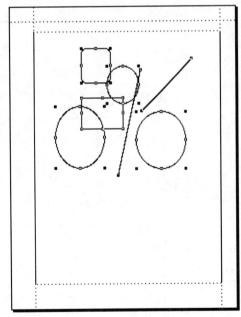

MOVING AND RESIZING GRAPHICS

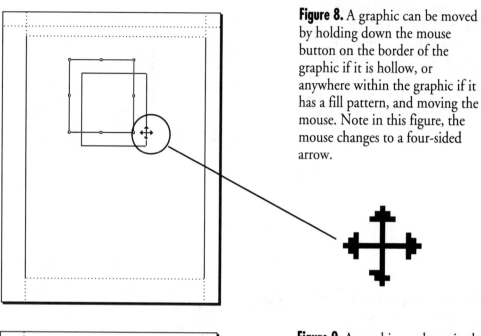

Figure 8. A graphic can be moved by holding down the mouse button on the border of the graphic if it is hollow, or anywhere within the graphic if it has a fill pattern, and moving the mouse. Note in this figure, the mouse changes to a four-sided arrow.

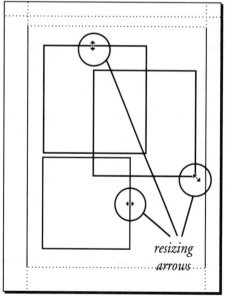

Figure 9. A graphic can be resized by grabbing one of the small black handles on its edge and dragging the mouse horizontally, vertically or diagonally.

resizing arrows

ALTERING THE APPEARANCE OF GRAPHICS

Figure 10. The **Element** menu includes both *Line* and *Fill* commands for altering the appearance of graphics.

Figure 11. To use the *Line* command, first select the graphic, go to the **Element** menu and select the *Line* command. When the sub-menu is activated, choose the desired line thickness.

In this figure, we are choosing 4 point line thickness.

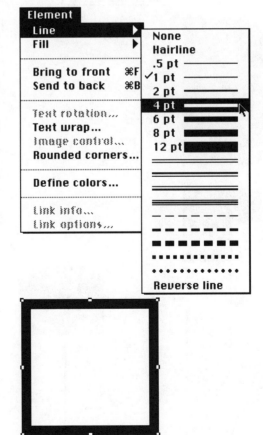

Figure 12. The graphic now adjusts to the new line thickness.

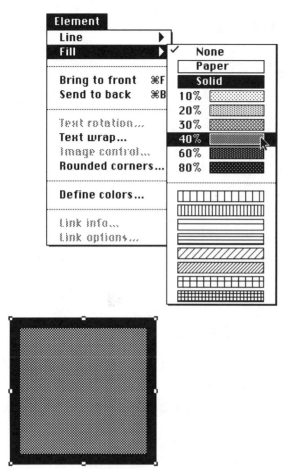

Figure 13. To change the fill of a graphic, select it, go to the **Element** menu and choose the *Fill* command. When the sub-menu appears, select the desired fill pattern.

In this figure, we are choosing a 40% fill.

Figure 14. The selected graphic will now reflect the new pattern or shade on screen.

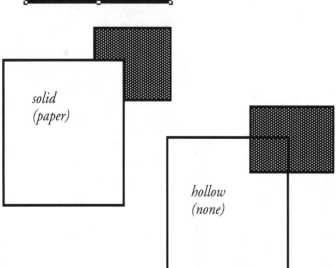

Figure 15. Note that a white graphic on screen can have a hollow or a solid fill.

The hollow fill is achieved by choosing *None* from the Figure 13 sub-menu. The solid fill is achieved by choosing *Paper* from the Figure 13 sub-menu.

Figure 16. These two graphics overlap each other. The gray is on top and the black on the bottom. We now want to reverse this situation.

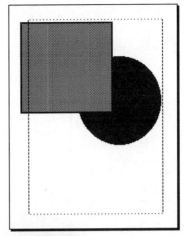

Figure 17. Select the top graphic and choose the *Send to back* command from the **Element** menu.

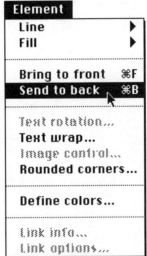

Figure 18. The black graphic is now on top.

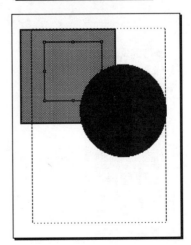

EDITING GRAPHICS

Figure 19. In the **Edit** menu, *Cut* removes a selected graphic from the screen to the Clipboard; *Copy* copies the selected graphic to the Clipboard and leaves the original graphic on screen; *Paste* transfers whatever is in the Clipboard back to the screen; *Clear* deletes a selected graphic from the screen, without transferring it to the Clipboard; and *Select all* selects all objects (graphics and text) on the screen.

SETTING GRAPHIC DEFAULTS

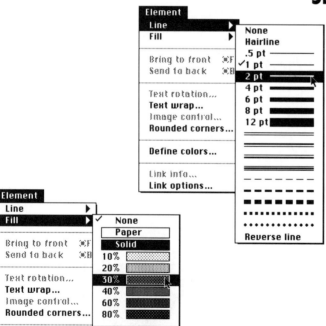

Figure 20. Choosing the *Line* or *Fill* command from the **Element** menu with the pointer tool (and no graphic selected), causes the particular *Line* or *Fill* selection to be the new default setting. This means that every new graphic you draw on the page will have these line and fill settings as their attributes.

CONSTRAINING GRAPHICS

Figure 21. The drawing of graphics may be constrained by use of the Shift key. This key, used with the square-corner, rounded-corner or oval drawing tool, constrains the object drawn to a square or circle, respectively. The Shift key, when used with the diagonal drawing tool, causes its operation to be the same as the perpendicular line drawing tool.

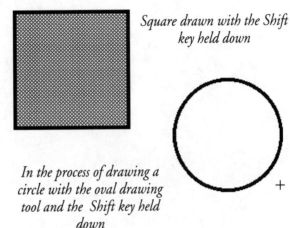

Square drawn with the Shift key held down

In the process of drawing a circle with the oval drawing tool and the Shift key held down

IMPORTING GRAPHICS

6

FORMATS PAGEMAKER SUPPORTS

PageMaker is able to import a wide variety of graphic files. These include bitmap files & scanned images (these can be paint or TIFF based files); PICT files (object oriented or vector based files) and EPS files (postscript coded files). Unless the graphic file is saved in one of these formats, PageMaker will not be able to place it within the document. Figures 1 through 4 provide examples of some of the different graphics possible to import.

Figure 1. A bitmap graphic from a paint program.

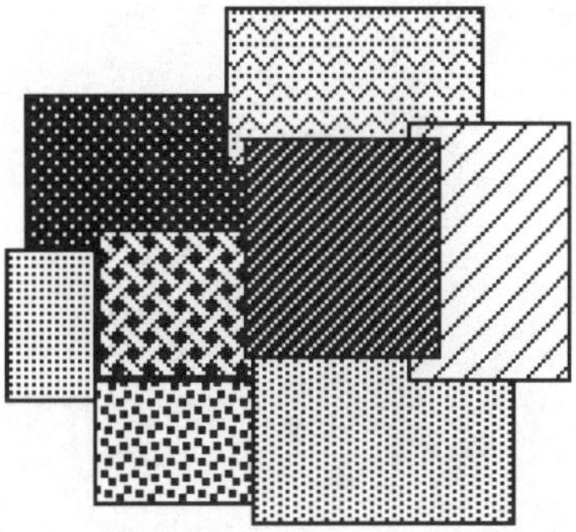

Figure 2. A PICT graphic.

Figure 3. An EPS graphic.

Figure 4. A scanned image.

LOADING GRAPHICS

Figure 5. The *Place* command within the **File** menu is used to import all graphics into PageMaker.

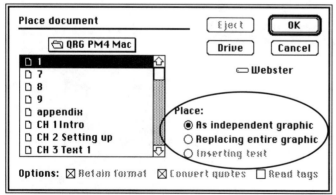

Figure 6. This is the *Place document* dialog box. The selections in the *Place:* options are applicable for two situations: you want to place a new graphic; or a current graphic is selected on the page, and you want to replace it with a new graphic.

Choose *As independent graphic:* if you wish to place a graphic independent of any other objects on the page.

See Figures 7 and 8 for further explanations.

Figure 7. *Replacing entire graphic:* If you first select a graphic on the page and then this option, the new graphic will replace the old one entirely, including any resizing and cropping that has been applied.

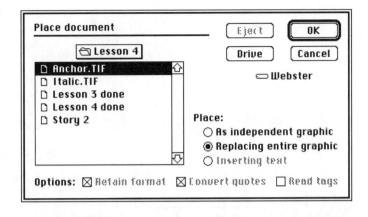

Figure 8. *As inline graphic:* If the text cursor is embedded in any text before you select the *Place* command, the graphic will be placed as an *Inline graphic*. See Figures 25 through 29 for more details.

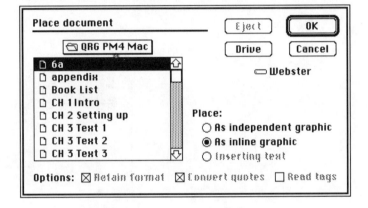

Figure 9. Depending upon the type of graphic being imported, the mouse cursor takes on one of the following four shapes:

(a) Paint type graphic;

(b) Object-oriented graphic;

(c) PostScript graphic; and

(d) scanned image.

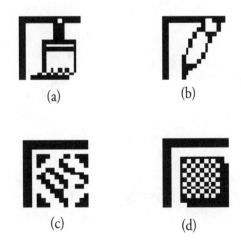

(a)　　　　(b)

(c)　　　　(d)

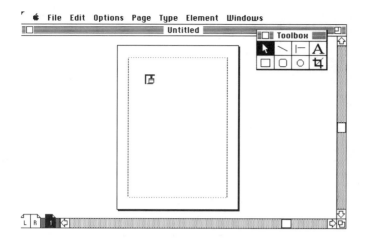

Figure 10. There are two ways to load a graphic onto the page. One way is to position the mouse cursor anywhere on screen and click once. By using this method, the graphic loads onto the page at its original size, which is often very difficult for you to judge until it has been loaded.

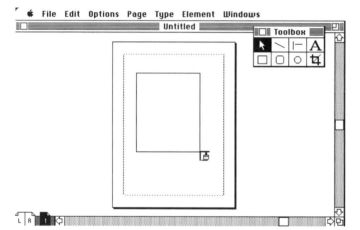

Figure 11. Another way to load a graphic is to draw an imaginary box the size you would like the graphic to be, while holding the mouse down.

Figure 12. Once the mouse button is released, the graphic will fill the area of the box. To resize the graphic proportionally, hold down the Shift key and select one of the corner handles to resize. The graphic will snap to its true proportions.

CROPPING GRAPHICS

Figure 13. The cropping tool crops imported graphics. Note how the cursor also changes to the same icon as the cropping tool.

Cropping tool

Cropping tool cursor

Figure 14. Select the graphic with the cropping tool and position this tool over one of the selected handles. Once the cursor changes to a two-headed arrow, move the mouse cursor towards the center of the graphic. This is similar to resizing a graphic, but in this case the graphic is cropped. Graphics can be cropped both horizontally and vertically.

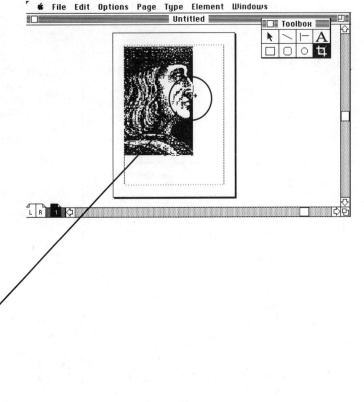

WRAPPING TEXT AROUND GRAPHICS

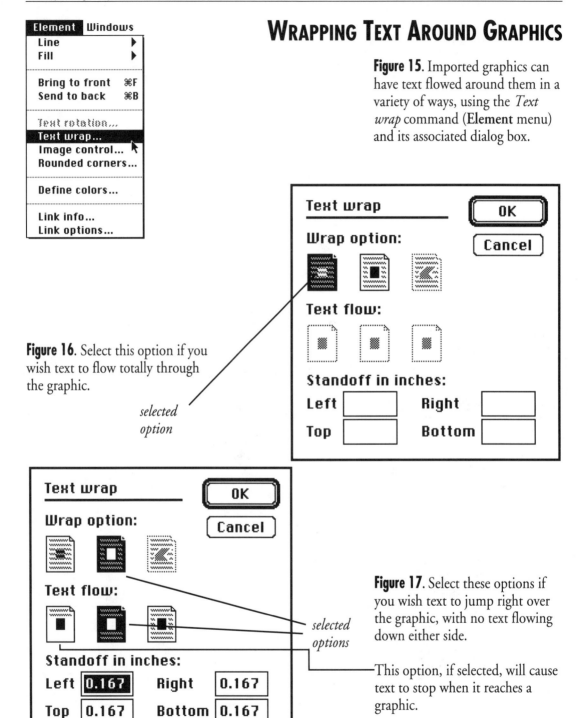

Figure 15. Imported graphics can have text flowed around them in a variety of ways, using the *Text wrap* command (**Element** menu) and its associated dialog box.

Figure 16. Select this option if you wish text to flow totally through the graphic.

selected option

selected options

Figure 17. Select these options if you wish text to jump right over the graphic, with no text flowing down either side.

This option, if selected, will cause text to stop when it reaches a graphic.

Figure 18. Select these options if you wish text to flow in a regular fashion around a graphic, including down both sides. See the example of Figure 19.

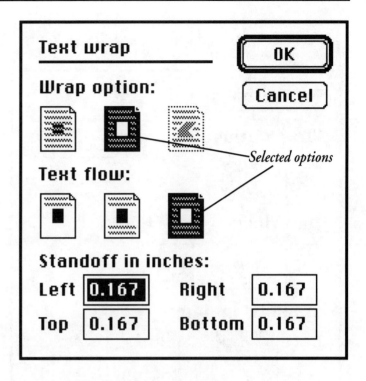

Figure 19. Example of text flowing regularly around a graphic. This was achieved with the *Text wrap* settings of Figure 18.

IRREGULAR WRAPAROUNDS

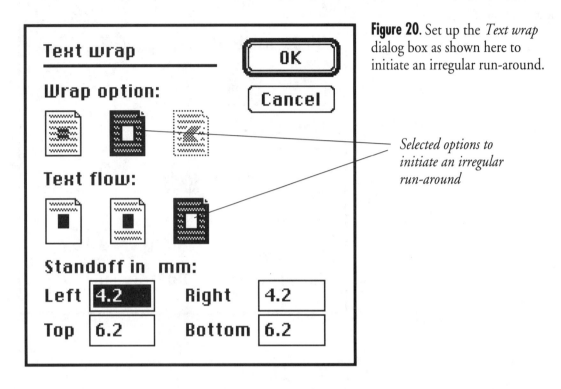

Figure 20. Set up the *Text wrap* dialog box as shown here to initiate an irregular run-around.

Selected options to initiate an irregular run-around

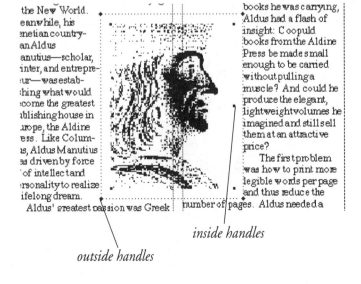

inside handles

outside handles

Figure 21. From the Figure 20 settings, two sets of handles will appear around the graphic. The inside handles resize the picture in the normal fashion. The outside handles are used to adjust the text wrap to any shape or configuration.

Figure 22. The outside handles can be moved with the mouse to adjust the shape of the wraparound, as we have started to do. Additional handles, to create more bends, can be added simply by clicking anywhere on the dotted lines with the mouse.

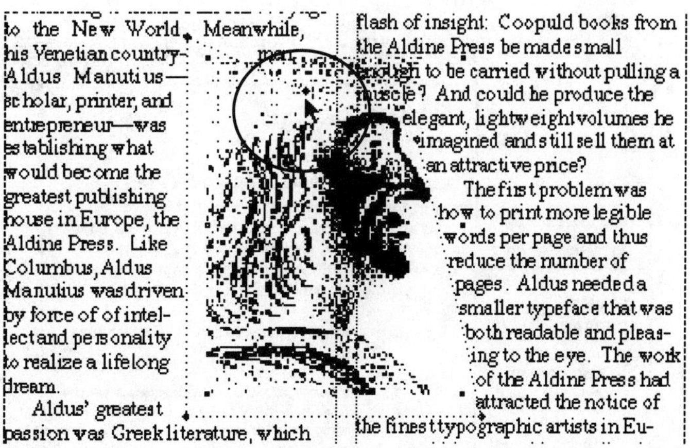

to the New World. Meanwhile, his Venetian country-Aldus Manutius—scholar, printer, and entrepreneur—was establishing what would become the greatest publishing house in Europe, the Aldine Press. Like Columbus, Aldus Manutius was driven by force of of intellect and personality to realize a lifelong dream. Aldus' greatest passion was Greek literature, which

flash of insight: Coopuld books from the Aldine Press be made small enough to be carried without pulling a muscle? And could he produce the elegant, lightweight volumes he imagined and still sell them at an attractive price? The first problem was how to print more legible words per page and thus reduce the number of pages. Aldus needed a smaller typeface that was both readable and pleasing to the eye. The work of the Aldine Press had attracted the notice of the finest typographic artists in Eu-

Figure 23. We created an extra handle by clicking in the top horizontal dotted line. This allowed the top right corner handle to be moved down towards the nose. Note how the text moves as the handles move. If you find it irritating having to wait for the text to reflow as you move each handle, move multiple handles while holding down the Spacebar. The text will not reflow until you release the Spacebar.

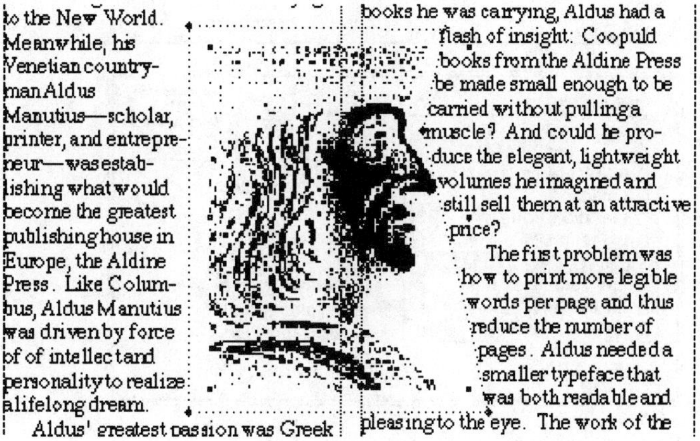

to the New World. Meanwhile, his Venetian countryman Aldus Manutius—scholar, printer, and entrepreneur—was establishing what would become the greatest publishing house in Europe, the Aldine Press. Like Columbus, Aldus Manutius was driven by force of of intellect and personality to realize a lifelong dream. Aldus' greatest passion was Greek

books he was carrying, Aldus had a flash of insight: Coopuld books from the Aldine Press be made small enough to be carried without pulling a muscle? And could he produce the elegant, lightweight volumes he imagined and still sell them at an attractive price? The first problem was how to print more legible words per page and thus reduce the number of pages. Aldus needed a smaller typeface that was both readable and pleasing to the eye. The work of the

Figure 24. A finished irregular runaround.

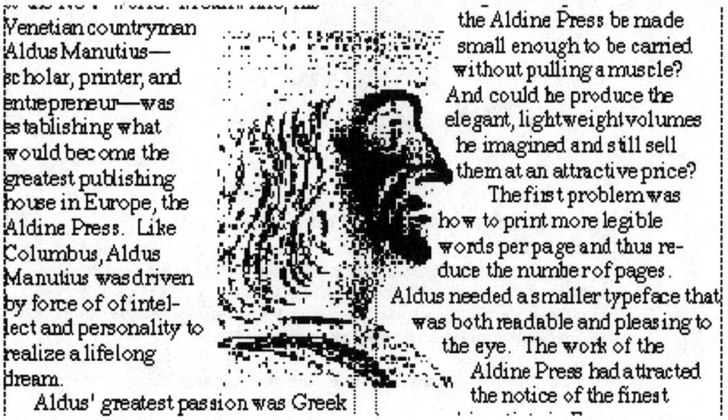

Venetian countryman Aldus Manutius—scholar, printer, and entrepreneur—was establishing what would become the greatest publishing house in Europe, the Aldine Press. Like Columbus, Aldus Manutius was driven by force of of intellect and personality to realize a lifelong dream. Aldus' greatest passion was Greek

the Aldine Press be made small enough to be carried without pulling a muscle? And could he produce the elegant, lightweight volumes he imagined and still sell them at an attractive price? The first problem was how to print more legible words per page and thus reduce the number of pages. Aldus needed a smaller typeface that was both readable and pleasing to the eye. The work of the Aldine Press had attracted the notice of the finest

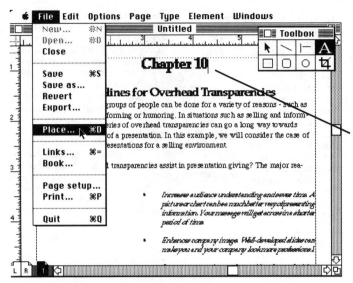

INLINE GRAPHICS

Inline graphics are graphics inserted as part of the text. As the text moves, they will move with it.

Figure 25. Inline graphics are created by inserting the text cursor in the text, and choosing the *Place* command from the **File** menu.

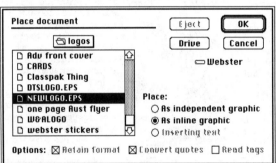

Figure 26. The *Place* command dialog box will automatically select the *As inline graphic* option, because the text cursor was inserted in the text.

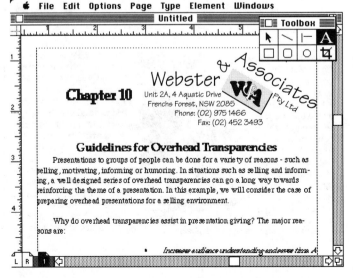

Figure 27. Clicking on OK in Figure 26 causes the graphic to be placed directly in the text. If the graphic is too big, resize it using the pointer tool in the normal way. This graphic will now move if the text is edited, or if the text is physically moved or resized with the pointer tool.

Figure 28. An independent graphic on the page can be turned into an inline graphic in your text as follows:

(a) Select the graphic (pointer tool).

(b) Choose *Cut* command (**Edit** menu).

(c) Place text cursor where graphic is required in text.

(d) Choose *Paste* command (**Edit** menu).

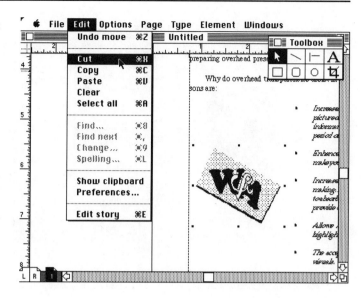

Figure 29. An inline graphic on your page can be turned into an independent graphic as follows:

(a) Select the graphic (pointer tool).

(b) Choose the *Cut* command (**Edit** menu).

(c) Choose the *Paste* command (**Edit** menu).

The graphic will re-appear in the text at the same location as when it was an inline graphic. However, it now can be selected by the pointer tool and moved independently.

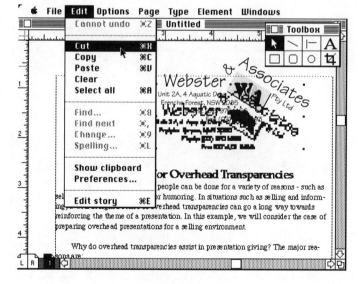

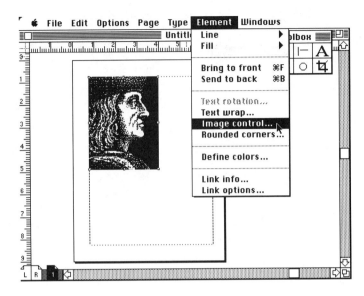

IMAGE CONTROL

Figure 30. Paint type packages and scanned images may have their appearance altered using the *Image control* command in the **Element** menu.

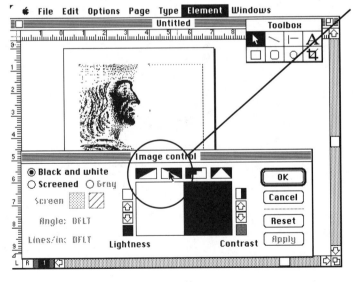

Figure 31. The *Image control* dialog box for a paint-type graphic. With *Black and white* selected, all you can do is invert the image by clicking on the rectangle in the dialog box as shown.

Figure 32. With *Screened* selected, the paint-type graphic can have its *Lightness* and *Contrast* adjusted, as well as its *Screen* type (dots or lines), *Angle* and *Lines/in.*

Clicking on the *Apply* button will show the graphic adjustments on the page without exiting the dialog box.

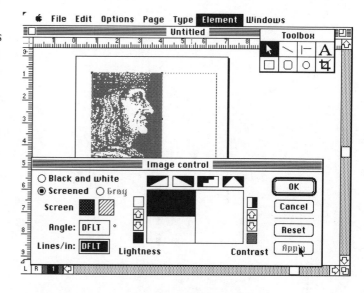

Figure 33. For scanned images, the dialog box can provide more precise manipulation of gray scale levels as shown in Figure 34.

Figure 34. More vertical bars indicate the additional gray scales available.

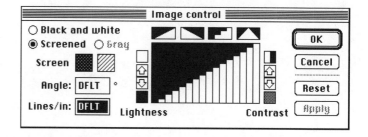

WORKING WITH TEMPLATES 7

CREATING TEMPLATES

A PageMaker template is like any other normal publication, except that it has a specific application as a 'dummy' document. A dummy document is one that may contain formatting information for a standard publication, such as a monthly newsletter. When a template is opened, it automatically opens a copy of the original document. This allows new information to be added to a document, knowing that it is already correctly formatted.

As you will see, below, a template may also contain text and graphics, and PageMaker provides a number of features for simple and easy replacement of these objects with new updated information.

Figure 1. A template is created in the same way as any other PageMaker publication. Add text and graphics as required, adjust the layout as needed, and use master page items, imported graphics etc., as you would for any document. The difference is in saving the file — the *Save* command from the **File** menu produces the *Save publication as* dialog box. In the right half of this box, click on the circle to the left of *Template* to create a template publication.

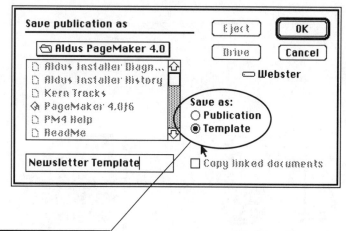

OPENING TEMPLATES

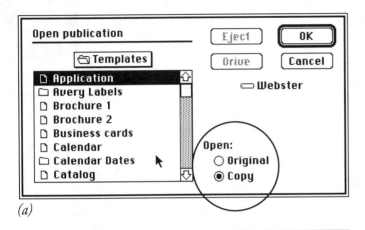

(a)

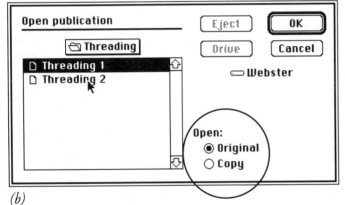

(b)

Figure 2. To open a template, use the *Open* command, as for any PageMaker publication. The dialog box automatically defaults to *Copy* as shown here. You may select *Original,* if you require, which is necessary if you wish to alter your original template.

Conversely, opening a normal publication, automatically defaults to *Original* as shown in (b). This also can be overridden to open a copy of a publication. **The only difference between a publication and a template is that a template automatically defaults to *Copy* when you are opening the publication.**

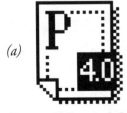

(a)

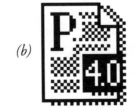

(b)

Figure 3. PageMaker templates and publications are easily distinguishable at the desktop level. Figure (a) shows the template icon, while Figure (b) shows the normal

USING TEMPLATES

Figure 4. When you open a copy of a template for modification, you need to be able to replace the text with that of your own choosing. This is done by selecting any part of the text file with the pointer tool (or inserting the text cursor anywhere within a story), and choosing the *Place* command from the **File** menu. If you wish to replace only part of a text file, that part is selected in its entirety with the text tool. In this figure, we have chosen a block of text in column one with the pointer tool.

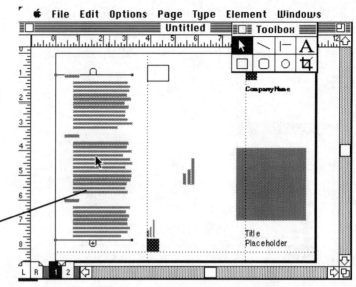

TEXT PLACEHOLDERS

Figure 5. The *Place document* dialog box gives you the option to choose *Replacing entire story,* which will now replace the total story selected in the template. If you had inserted the text cursor in the text, then the *Inserting text* option could also have been selected. If you had selected, with the text tool, a portion of text, a new option—*Replacing selected text*— would have appeared for selection. With these methods, new text stories can quickly and easily replace earlier outdated stories. The old and new text stories do not need to be of the same length.

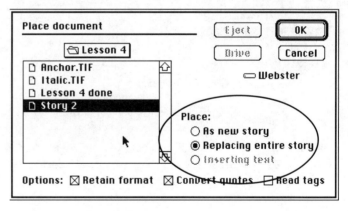

The text, contained within the original template, is called a text placeholder.

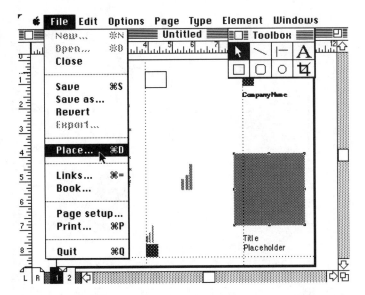

GRAPHIC PLACEHOLDERS

Figure 6. Replacing old graphics with new imported graphics is even simpler than replacing text. Select the graphic you wish to replace with the pointer tool, and choose the *Place* command again (**File** menu).

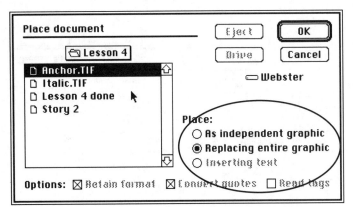

Figure 7. The *Place* command dialog box gives you the option of choosing the *Replacing entire graphic* selection, or *As independent graphic*. The latter choice is for loading graphics in the normal way. The former choice is the one to select. Click on OK, and it immediately loads the graphic over the selected graphic on your page. The same graphic size and parameters are kept, including cropping and text wraparound attributes. These can be changed if necessary.

The graphic contained within the original template is called a graphic placeholder.

PageMaker Defaults

Application and Publication Defaults

PageMaker is shipped with preset options for many of its settings. These may differ between US, International English and other foreign language settings. PageMaker includes two kinds of defaults: *Application* and *Publication*. *Application* defaults are wide-ranging, and apply to every publication that you open. They are setup at the desktop level, before you enter a new or pre-saved publication. *Publication* defaults only apply to the currently open publication.

APPLICATION DEFAULTS

If you wish to have the same settings for every new PageMaker file, then the *Application* default approach is the way to go. For example, the number of columns by default is pre-set to 1. If you wish to change this to 3 columns, you would alter this at the desktop (see Figure 1).

Figure 1. To change *Application* defaults, open PageMaker by double-clicking on the PageMaker icon (or choose *Close* from the **File** menu if inside PageMaker). You will then be at the PageMaker 4 desktop level. Normally, at this level, you choose, through the **File** menu to select *New*, or *Open* to select a previously saved publication.

  Before doing this, you can change any default setting which will then apply to all new publications, until changed at the desktop again. Here we are changing the *Column guides* options to 3.

|  | File | Edit | **Options** | Page | Type | Element | Windows |

Column guides

OK
Cancel

Number of columns: 3
Space between columns: 4.2 mm

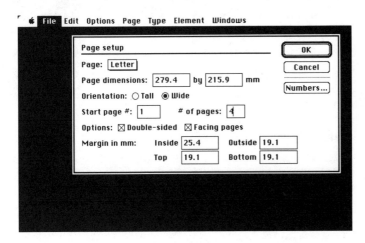

Figure 2. In this figure, we are setting up, at the PageMaker desktop, a new default for the way a new PageMaker document will open. We are setting this, through the *Page setup* command (**File** menu), to *Letter, Wide* and *# of pages* at 4.

All new documents will now open with these parameters as standard.

To determine which options can be set and changed at the PageMaker desktop, check each menu in turn. All commands in black can be selected and altered (except of course *New, Open* and *Quit,* which have pre-set defined roles within PageMaker).

Those commands in gray cannot be selected at the desktop. Every command in the **Page** menu, for example, is grayed out. Such commands are not associated with default settings, and are applicable to manipulating an actual publication.

PUBLICATION DEFAULTS

Publication defaults are different to *Application* defaults in that they
are set up inside an already open publication, and apply to that
publication only. (Publication defaults can be used to override
Application defaults.) For example, you may wish to change the
default text option for typing text within a single publication.
Normally this is set by default, at Times 12 point. You can easily
change it for this publication to, say, Palatino 12 point, without
affecting how PageMaker will open up for other new publications (see
Figure 3).

Figure 3. *Publication* defaults are
those which are changed inside
the publication only. Any changes
to these defaults are only
applicable to the publicat-ion in
which they are changed.

For example, inside a publication in this figure, we are adjusting
the default text type to be
Palatino at 12 point. Again, any
default setting can be adjusted this
way. When you do this, ensure
that the pointer tool is active, and
no other object (text or graphics)
is selected on the page.

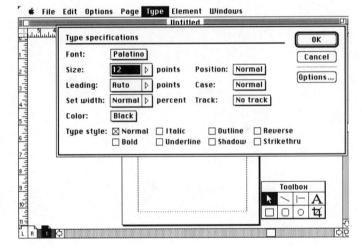

USING STYLE SHEETS 9

WHAT IS A STYLE SHEET?

A style sheet is defined by a list of style names that appear in the *Style palette*. These names are given specific character descriptions, which can be applied to text in a PageMaker document. The styles can be copied from one publication to another.

Figure 1. PageMaker's style sheet approach provides a number of style names, containing text attribute descriptions, that can be applied to paragraphs of text. The styles available are contained in the *Style palette* accessed through the **Windows** menu. By default, PageMaker includes the style names shown in the *Style palette* of this figure.

Figure 2. Applying a style to text means all the text attribute definitions chosen for that style name will be applied to the selected text. In Figure 2 (a) we have inserted the cursor in the top paragraph and are about to click on the *Headline* style. Figure 2 (b) shows the immediate result.

The paragraph now takes on the text attributes defined under the Headline style name.

(a)

(b)

CREATING STYLES

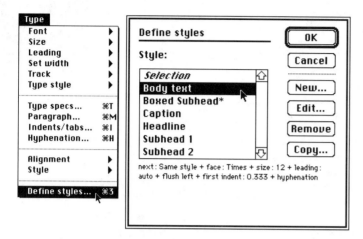

Figure 3. You create new style names by first selecting the *Define styles* command from the **Type** menu. The *Define styles* dialog box appears. The middle rectangle lists the different style names currently available.

Clicking in any style will list its specifications at the bottom of the dialog box. Clicking on the *New* button allows a new style to be created. This results in the *Edit style* dialog box of Figure 4.

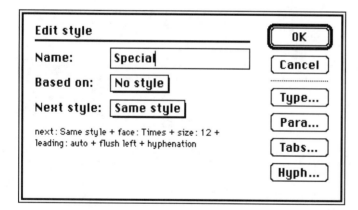

Figure 4. From the *Edit style* dialog box you can create a new style. Type the name of the new style in the *Name:* rectangle. We have typed in the word 'Special'. The four commands at the right: *Type, Para, Tabs, Hyph,* allow for a variety of text specifications to be set for any new style. Click on the button you require. See Figures 5 through 9 for more details.

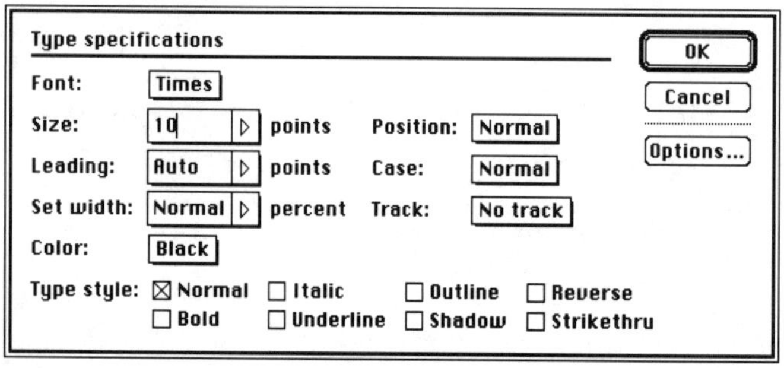

Figure 5. This is the *Type specifications* dialog box, obtained from clicking on the *Type* button in Figure 4. Choose any attributes you like and click on OK. You are then returned back to Figure 4. This dialog box is identical to that described in Figure 12, Chapter 3, **Working with Text.**

Figure 6. This is the *Paragraph specifications* dialog box, obtained from clicking on the *Para* button in Figure 4. Clicking on OK, once modifying any specifications, returns you back to Figure 4. The options available in this dialog box are explained starting at Figure 16 in Chapter 3, **Working with Text**.

Figure 7. This is the *Indents/tabs* dialog box, obtained from clicking on the *Tabs* button in Figure 4. Clicking on OK once modified, returns you back to Figure 4. This dialog box is explained commencing at Figure 41 in Chapter 3, **Working with Text**.

Figure 8. The *Hyphenation* dialog box, obtained from clicking on the *Hyph* button in Figure 4. Clicking on OK once modified, returns you back to Figure 4. This dialog box is discussed, starting at Figure 50 in Chapter 3, **Working with Text**.

Figure 9. The *Define styles* dialog box after modifications as shown in the Figures 5 through 8 dialog boxes. Note the style 'Special' is now included and highlighted in the List. The attributes given to the Special style are displayed here.

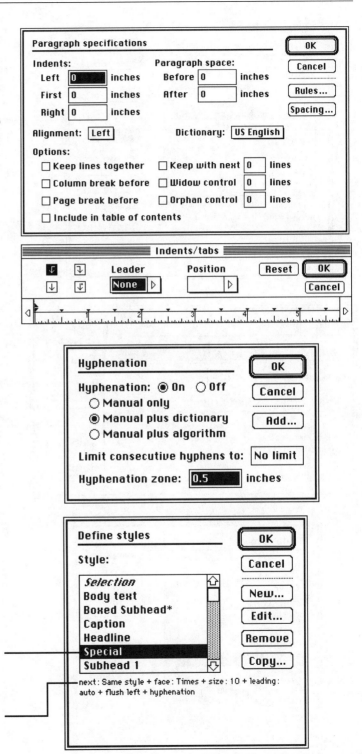

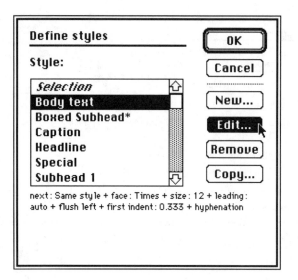

EDITING STYLES

Figure 10. One of the major advantages of using style names with text, is that it is very simple to change the attributes of a large amount of text by simply changing the specifications of the style. Any paragraphs applied this style will automatically change to the new specifications. To edit a style, you start with the *Define styles* dialog box of Figure 10 and click on the *Edit* button as shown here.

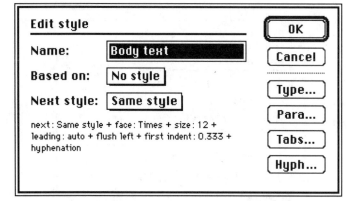

Figure 11. From the action of Figure 10, the *Edit style* dialog box will appear. As Body text was selected in Figure 10, its name is automatically included in Figure 11. This style can now be edited using the *Type, Para, Tabs* and *Hyph* buttons in an identical fashion as discussed above (Figures 5 through 8) for creating a new style.

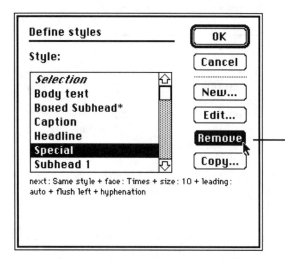

Figure 12. Removing a style is very simple. Click on the style name in the *Define styles* dialog box (in our case 'Special'), and click on *Remove.*

OTHER WAYS TO ADD STYLES

Figure 13. It is possible to add a new style which is based upon a currently named style. Click on a style name (in our case Body text) and then click on *New* in the *Define styles* dialog box.

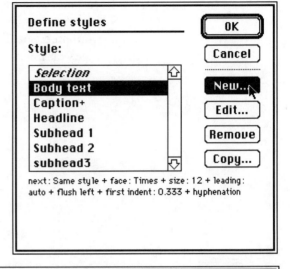

Figure 14. The *Edit style* dialog box will appear and will now include the name Body text in the *Based on*: box. The new style name you are defining (say Body text 2) will now start off with the same attributes as Body text. You may make any necessary changes to Body text 2 using the same approach as outlined in Figures 5 through 8.

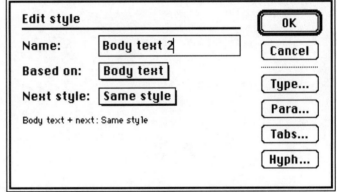

Figure 15. Styles may also be copied from other publications. Simply choose the *Copy* command from the *Define styles* dialog box, and then choose the publication from the list of publications that will appear.

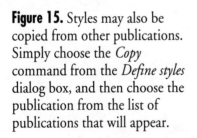

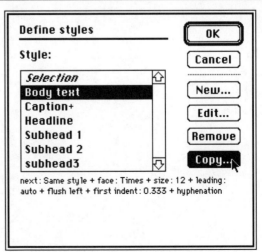

Style names may also be imported from word processing documents. In addition, you may also define style names in angle brackets (<>), at the beginning of a paragraph, inside you word processor. These will then come across into your PageMaker document correctly named with the correct style.

USING COLOR

CREATING AND EDITING COLORS

PageMaker supports the full range of Pantone colors. Defining individual colors is also possible.

Figure 1. To use colors within PageMaker, the *Color palette* must be visible on screen. This palette can be turned on or off via the *Color palette* command in the **Windows** menu. It can also be closed by clicking in the *Close* box in its top left-hand corner.

Figure 2. You create new colors by selecting the *Define colors* command from the **Element** menu to activate the *Define colors* dialog box. The larger rectangle lists the various colors currently defined; these include the default values provided with PageMaker 4. Clicking on the *New* button allows a new color to be created. This results in the *Edit color* dialog box of Figure 3.

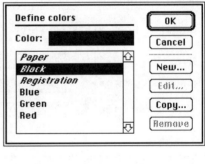

Figure 3. From the *Edit color* dialog box you create a new color. Type in the name in the *Name:* rectangle. You then have a choice of which color model to use: RGB, HLS, CMYK or Pantone. By adjusting the color percentages using any of the first three methods, the top half of the color rectangle in the bottom right of the dialog box constantly changes to reflect the new color (see Figures 4 through 6). Figure 7 explains the Pantone option.

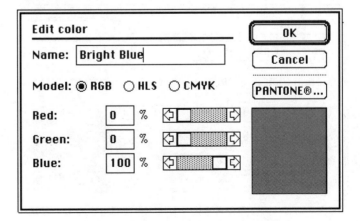

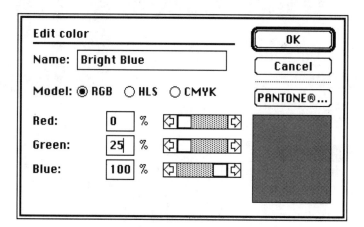

Figure 4. The RGB method allows you to define a color by varying the percentages of these three colors.

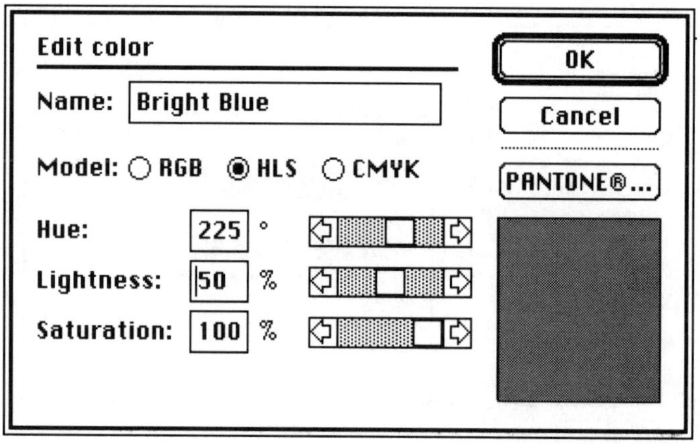

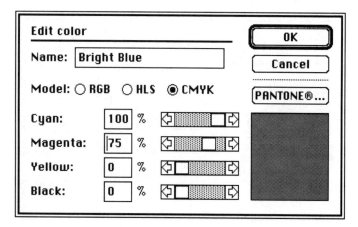

Figure 5. The HLS model is similar to RGB, but Hue is defined in degrees from 0 to 360.

Figure 6. The CMYK model utilizes percentages of Cyan, Magenta, Yellow and Black to define colors.

Figure 7. The Pantone color can be accessed by clicking on the *Pantone* button from the Figure 3 *Edit color* dialog box. This activates the *PANTONE Color* dialog box shown here. Pantone colors are chosen by using the scroll bar to find the one required, and then clicking on it with the mouse. Alternatively, if you know the color, enter the name or number directly into the PANTONE rectangle at the top of the dialog box.

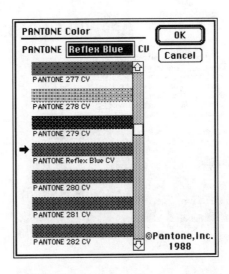

Figure 8. After defining the color using any of the above methods, click on OK in the Figure 3 *Edit color* dialog box to return to the *Define colors* dialog box again. This figure shows the new color, defined in Figure 3, now appearing in the color name list. This name will also now appear in the *Color palette* of Figure 1.

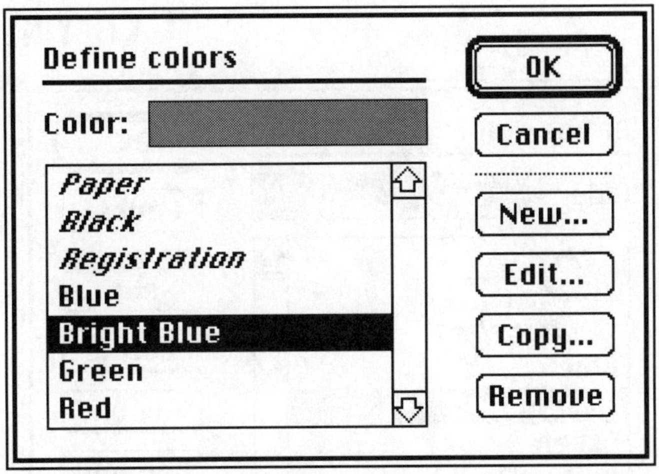

Figure 9. Colors are edited in a similar fashion to the way they are created. The *Edit color* dialog box allows any color to be changed at any time. This dialog box is entered by clicking on the *Edit* button of the *Define colors* dialog box of Figures 2 or 8. Make sure you first select the color you wish to edit. Note that you cannot edit the default colors of Black and Registration.

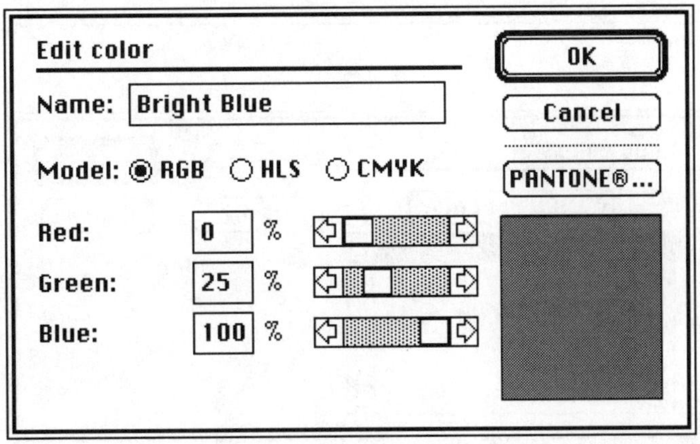

APPLYING COLOR TO TEXT AND GRAPHICS

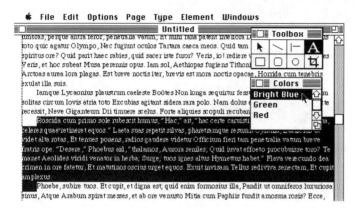

Figure 10. Color can be applied to text or graphics. First select the object and choose the color required from the *Color palette*. In this figure we have selected a paragraph, and are applying the Bright Blue color through the *Color palette.*

COPYING AND REMOVING COLORS

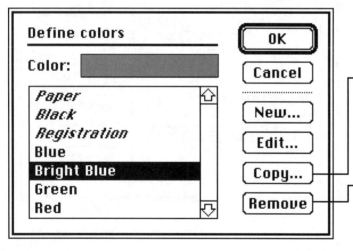

Figure 11. Two other buttons in the *Define colors* dialog box are available. To copy colors from other publications, click on the *Copy* button and then select the relevant document from the dialog box that appears (Figure 12).

To remove a color, highlight it and click on the *Remove* button.

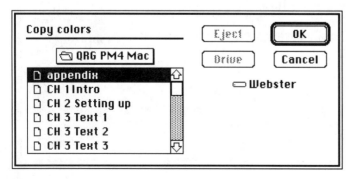

Figure 12. This is the *Copy colors* dialog box that is activated after clicking on the *Copy* button of Figure 11. From here, select the file you wish to copy the colors from.

PRINTING

PRINT DIALOG BOX

All printing preferences are set in the *Print* dialog box activated through the *Print* command.

Figure 1. Once you have a publication that is ready to print, you select the *Print* command from the **File** menu.

File
New...	⌘N
Open...	⌘O
Close	
Save	⌘S
Save as...	
Revert	
Export...	
Place...	⌘D
Links...	⌘=
Book...	
Page setup...	
Print...	⌘P
Quit	⌘Q

Figure 2. On selecting the *Print* command from the **File** menu, you will be confronted with the *Print to:* dialog box.

The *Copies:* option lets you specify the amount of times your publication will be printed. You may enter any figure between 1 and 100 in the associated figure box (which by default will be on 1 and displayed in reverse video.)

Print to: Newgen Image 5000

Copies: **1** ☐ Collate ☐ Reverse order

Page range: ◉ All ○ From `1` to `1`

Paper source: ◉ Paper tray ○ Manual feed

Scaling: `100` % ☐ Thumbnails, `16` per page

Book: ○ Print this pub only ○ Print entire book

Printer: `General`   Paper: `A4`
Size: 210.0 X 297.0 mm   Tray: ◉ Select
Print area: 210.0 X 297.0 mm

[Print]
[Cancel]
[Options...]
[PostScript...]

Figure 3. The *Collate* option is used when you are printing multiple copies of a publication that contains more than one page. If it is a document with many graphics, it may be faster to collate it manually.

Print to: Newgen Image 5000

Copies: **1** ☐ Collate ☐ Reverse order

Page range: ◉ All ○ From `1` to `1`

Paper source: ◉ Paper tray ○ Manual feed

Scaling: `100` % ☐ Thumbnails, `16` per page

Book: ○ Print this pub only ○ Print entire book

Printer: `General`   Paper: `A4`
Size: 210.0 X 297.0 mm   Tray: ◉ Select
Print area: 210.0 X 297.0 mm

[Print]
[Cancel]
[Options...]
[PostScript...]

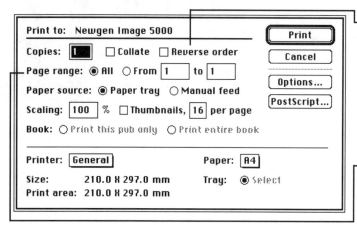

Figure 4. The *Reverse order* option, once selected, will print your pages in the opposite order to what your printer would have printed them, either first to last or last to first.

The *Page range:* option lets you select all or some of your document to print. Clicking the mouse inside the *All* option will print the whole publication. Clicking on the *From* option lets you specify which section of the publication that you would like to print.

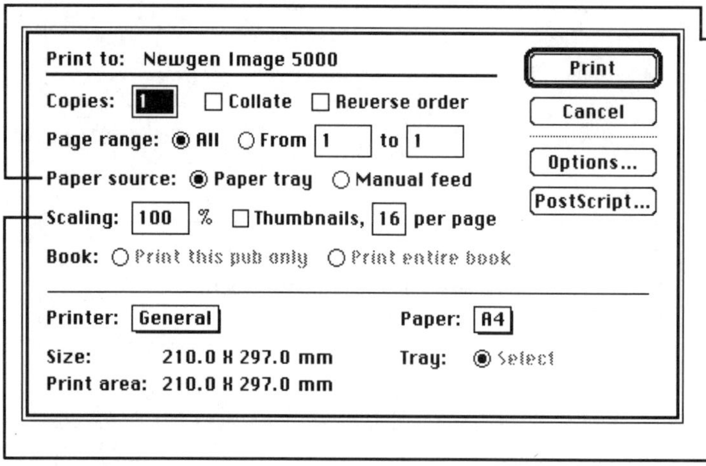

Figure 5. The *Paper source* option has two choices available for the placement of your paper. The first choice is *Paper tray.* If you have this option selected, the paper in your printer will be taken from the paper tray. If you select the *Manual feed* option, the paper will have to be fed into the printer manually.

The *Scaling:* option lets you scale your page, within a range of 25 to 1,000 percent.

Figure 6. The *Thumbnails* option will print a miniature version of your publication on one page, or depending on the size of your publication, a minimal number of pages. The default setting is 16, which means 16 miniature pages will appear on each page. Up to 64 *Thumbnails* can be printed per page.

The *Book* option can only be selected if the document you have open is part of, or contains a *Book list* (see Chapter 12 **Book List**). You have two choices here; to print the currently open publication, or its entire *Book list*.

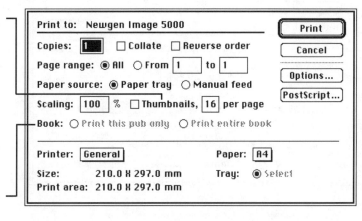

Figure 7. At the bottom of the Print dialog box are the *Printer* and *Paper* selections. Use these to adjust your printer type and/or paper size.

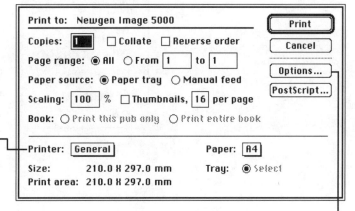

PRINT OPTIONS

Figure 8. The *Options* button under the *Cancel* button in the *Print to* dialog box activates the *Aldus print options* dialog box shown here.

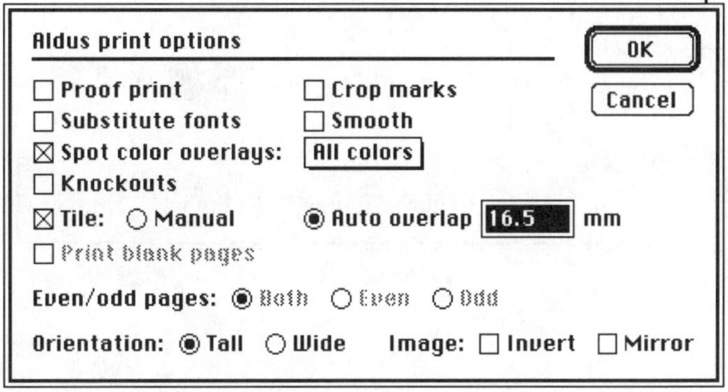

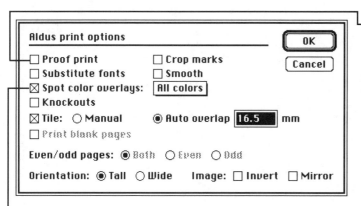

Figure 9. The *Proof print* option will only print text and graphics created in PageMaker. All imported graphics will be substituted with a diagonal cross.

The *Substitute fonts* option, on being selected, will swap the printer fonts for screen fonts.

Figure 10. The *Spot color overlays* option will print a separate page for each color you have used in your publication. Use this feature when you want your publication to be commercially printed. The sub-menu of the *Spot color overlays* option, which is activated by holding the mouse on it, gives you the option of printing overlays for all colors in your publication, or just a selected one.

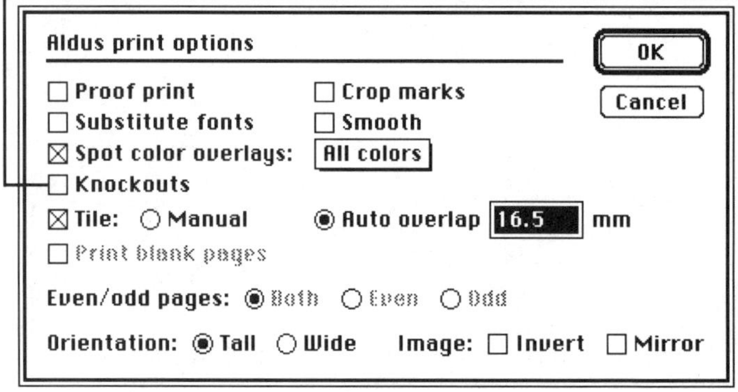

Figure 11. The *Knockouts* option can only be selected when you are printing spot color overlays. Any colored sections on your page that overlap will be printed as a blank area.

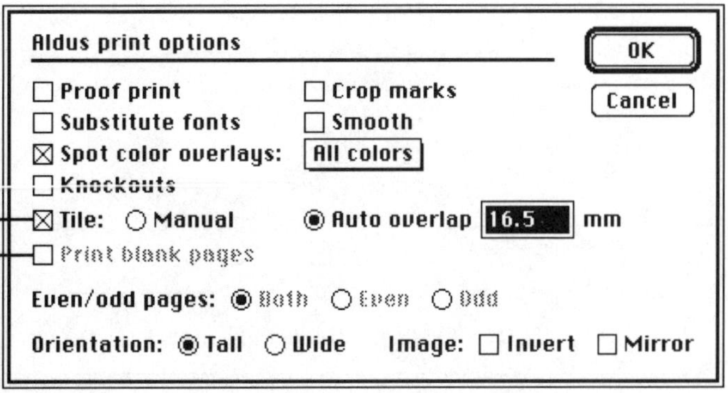

Figure 12. The *Tile* option will allow you to print a page or pages, that are larger than the printer is capable, on separate pages that can be tiled together and slightly overlapped. The amount of image or page that will overlap is set in the *Auto overlap* figure box. Selecting *Manual* for this option lets you determine how much of the image or page will actually overlap.

If your publication contains any blank pages that you want printed, select the *Print blank pages* option.

Figure 13. On selecting the *Crop marks* option, PageMaker will place crop marks in all four corners of the page. If you are printing a Letter size page on Letter size paper, crop marks will obviously not appear.

The *Smooth* option will smooth out the edges of rough looking graphics that have been imported into PageMaker. This will provide better printed output.

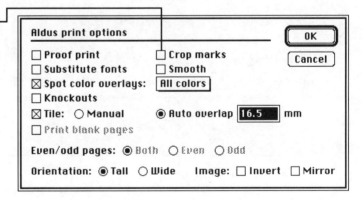

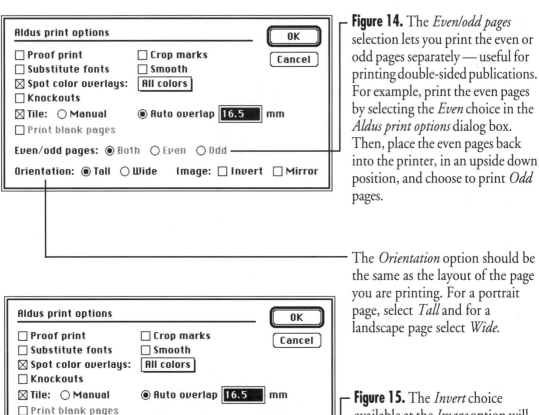

Figure 14. The *Even/odd pages* selection lets you print the even or odd pages separately — useful for printing double-sided publications. For example, print the even pages by selecting the *Even* choice in the *Aldus print options* dialog box. Then, place the even pages back into the printer, in an upside down position, and choose to print *Odd* pages.

The *Orientation* option should be the same as the layout of the page you are printing. For a portrait page, select *Tall* and for a landscape page select *Wide*.

Figure 15. The *Invert* choice available at the *Image* option will print a negative image of your page. The *Mirror* image will print a reversed image.

POSTSCRIPT PRINT OPTIONS

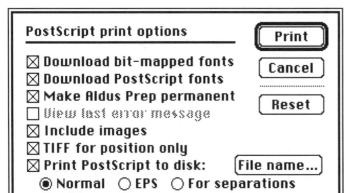

Figure 16. The *PostScript print options* dialog box is obtained by selecting the *PostScript* button under the *Options* button in the *Print to* dialog box of Figure 2.

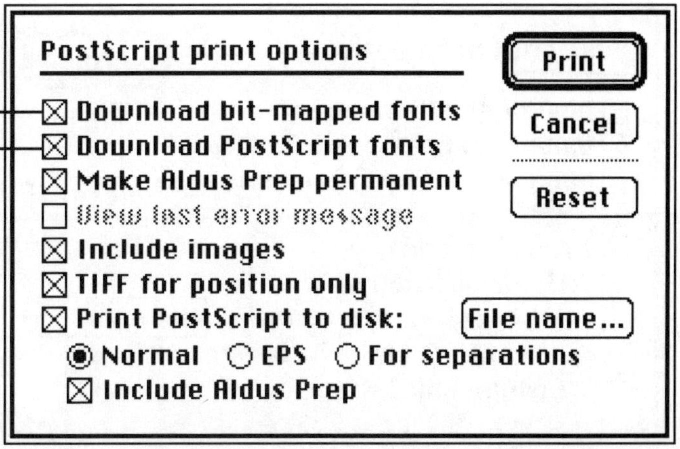

Figure 17. When selecting the *Download bit-mapped fonts* option, PageMaker will download bit-mapped fonts to the printer when PostScript fonts cannot be found.

The *Download PostScript fonts* option will download any PostScript fonts on your page that are not available in your printer.

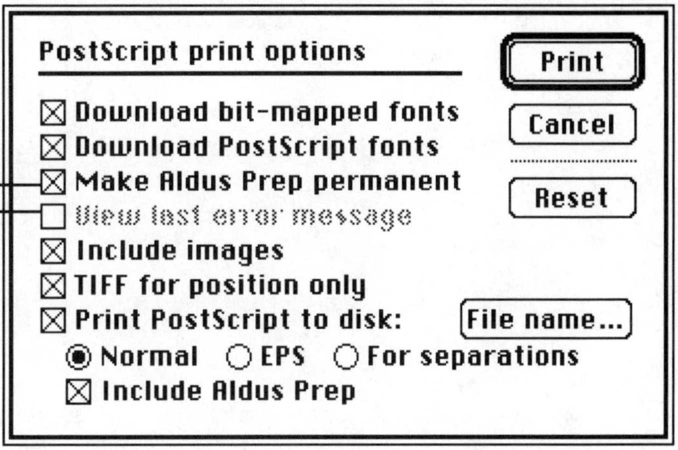

```
PostScript print options                    [ Print  ]

⊠ Download bit-mapped fonts                 [ Cancel ]
⊠ Download PostScript fonts
⊠ Make Aldus Prep permanent                 [ Reset  ]
☐ View last error message
⊠ Include images
⊠ TIFF for position only
⊠ Print PostScript to disk:        [ File name... ]
  ● Normal   ○ EPS   ○ For separations
  ⊠ Include Aldus Prep
```

Figure 18. *Make Aldus Prep permanent.* This option, when checked, will make *Aldus Prep* a permanent fixture in your printer until turned off.

The *View last error message* option will display messages concerning any printing problems you may be having.

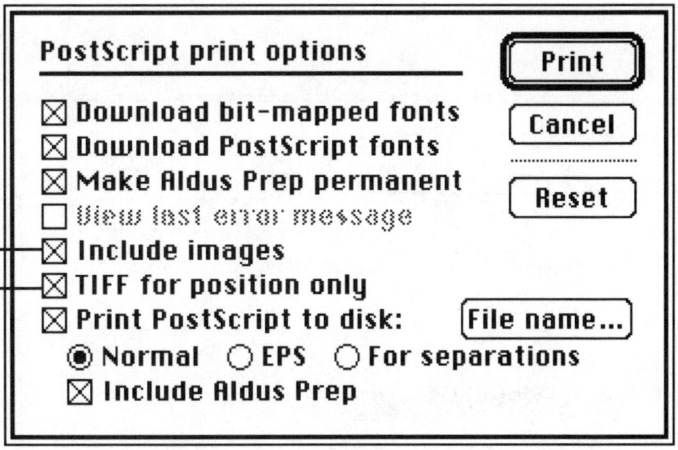

```
PostScript print options                    [ Print  ]

⊠ Download bit-mapped fonts                 [ Cancel ]
⊠ Download PostScript fonts
⊠ Make Aldus Prep permanent                 [ Reset  ]
☐ View last error message
⊠ Include images
⊠ TIFF for position only
⊠ Print PostScript to disk:        [ File name... ]
  ● Normal   ○ EPS   ○ For separations
  ⊠ Include Aldus Prep
```

Figure 19. The *Include images* option, when checked, will print your document, page or publication with any images that were imported into PageMaker.

TIFF for position only. When you have this option selected, your PageMaker document will be printed with all TIFF images at a lower resolution.

```
PostScript print options                    [ Print  ]

⊠ Download bit-mapped fonts                 [ Cancel ]
⊠ Download PostScript fonts
⊠ Make Aldus Prep permanent                 [ Reset  ]
☐ View last error message
⊠ Include images
⊠ TIFF for position only
⊠ Print PostScript to disk:        [ File name... ]
  ● Normal   ○ EPS   ○ For separations
  ⊠ Include Aldus Prep
```

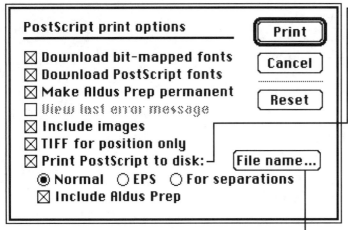

Figure 20. If you want your PageMaker document to be printed to a disk and not to a printer, select the *Print PostScript to disk* option. The reasons for printing your PageMaker file to a disk becomes apparent when you see the choices available with this option. The *Normal* option is selected if your publication contains multiple pages, or if the printer you are using is in a different location. It is also used if you use a service bureau for printing.

The *EPS* option will convert a single page of your publication into an EPS file for use in PageMaker and other programs that accept EPS files.

The *For separations* option will prepare the document to be used in a program that prints full color separations.

If the printer that is going to be used to print this file does not contain *Aldus Prep*, select this option.

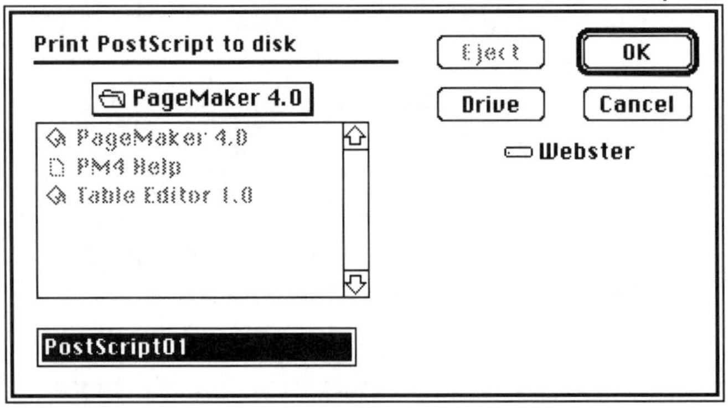

Figure 21. If you are going to use the option of printing a PostScript file to disk, you must also select the *File name* option. On clicking your mouse on this button, a *Print PostScript to disk* dialog box will appear, where you will give the file a name and decide where to save it. Here we have clicked on the *File name* button with the *Normal* option selected.

ASSEMBLING A BOOK 12

BOOK COMMAND

PageMaker's *Book* command allows multiple PageMaker publications to be linked together to form one large document. Using the *Book* command allows you to list the names of all publications that form part of a total document. Many chapters may be automatically linked together to form a complete book.

Figure 1. Using the book command, it is possible to produce a table of contents and an index which contain multiple publications, and to print these multiple publications as one book.

```
File
New...         ⌘N
Open...         ⌘O
Close

Save            ⌘S
Save as...
Revert
Export...

Place...        ⌘D

Links...        ⌘=
Book...

Page setup...
Print...        ⌘P

Quit            ⌘Q
```

GENERATING A BOOK LIST

Figure 2. The *Book publication list* dialog box appears from invoking the *Book* command of Figure 1. The *Book list* rectangle, to the right of this box, is where the names of the different publications are added to complete the *Book list*. The rectangle to the left allows you to search through your PageMaker publications on disk, to find the documents to add to the *Book list*. See Figure 3 for details on how to actually compile this list.

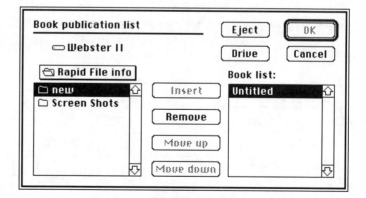

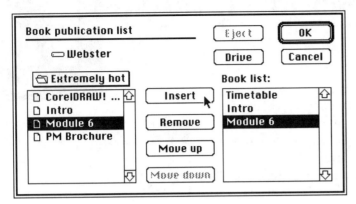

Figure 3. The *Book list* rectangle is added to by clicking on a specific publication listed on the left, and then clicking on the *Insert* button. The publication is then placed in the *Book list*. Repeat this procedure for all required publications. An alternative method for adding publications to the *Book list* is to double-click on the name of the publication in the left-hand rectangle. It will then be automatically added to the *Book list*.

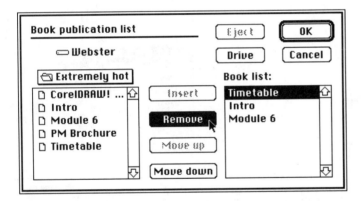

Figure 4. Documents can be easily removed from the *Book list*. Simply click on the name you wish to delete and then click on the *Remove* button. The publication is automatically deleted from the list.

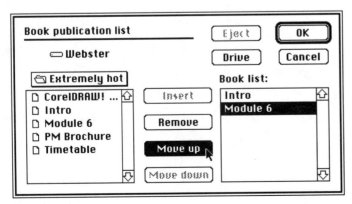

Figure 5. It is important to ensure that the list of publications in the *Book list* are in the correct order. This order can be changed by using the *Move up* and *Move down* buttons. Highlight the publications that you wish to move, and click on the *Move up* or *Move down* keys, as required.

PRINTING A BOOK LIST

Figure 6. The *Print to* dialog box (*Print* command in the **File** menu) allows you the option of printing a single publication or the entire *Book list*. To print the entire list, click in the *Print entire book* option in this dialog box.

```
Print to:  Webster & Associates              [  Print  ]

Copies:  [1]    □ Collate  □ Reverse order   [  Cancel  ]
Page range:  ⊙ All  ○ From [1]   to [1]
                                             [ Options... ]
Paper source:  ⊙ Paper tray  ○ Manual feed
                                             [ PostScript... ]
Scaling: [100] %  □ Thumbnails, [16] per page

Book:  ○ Print this pub only  ⊙ Print entire book

Printer: [General]              Paper: [A4]
Size:        210.0 H 297.0 mm   Tray:  ⊙ Select
Print area:  210.0 H 297.0 mm
```

Note: A Book list need only be created in one publication of the total book. It is not important which publication you choose for this, but obviously all the publications will need to be created prior to this procedure. It is possible for a publication to appear in more than one Book list.

TABLES OF CONTENTS

13

DEFINING CONTENTS STYLES

To generate a Table of Contents in PageMaker it is important to have pre-defined the styles that will be searched for. This prerequisite must be carried out in the *Paragraph specifications* dialog box.

Figure 1. PageMaker 4 generates a table of contents based upon the way you set up the different paragraph styles. Depending upon whether you have defined a style to be included in the table of contents (see Figure 2), PageMaker will only search for these paragraphs as it generates its contents.

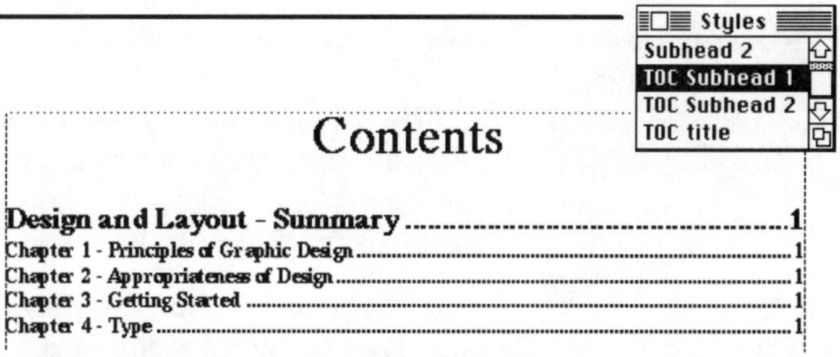

Figure 2. In the *Paragraph specifications* dialog box (**Type** menu), at the very bottom, is the option *Include in table of contents*. If this option is checked while you are creating a style, all the paragraphs which include this style, will form part of the generated contents. Many different styles within a publication may have this option checked as part of their style's definition.

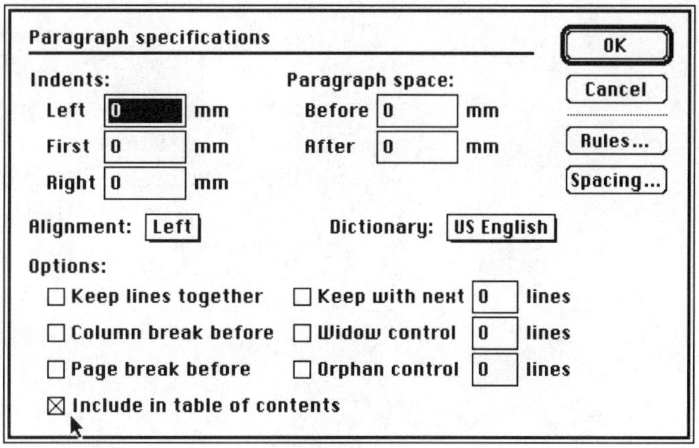

GENERATING CONTENTS

Figure 3. To generate the table of contents, you first choose the *Create TOC* command in the **Options** menu.

Styles
Subhead 2
TOC Subhead 1
TOC Subhead 2
TOC title

Contents

Design and Layout – Summary 1
Chapter 1 - Principles of Graphic Design 1
Chapter 2 - Appropriateness of Design 1
Chapter 3 - Getting Started 1
Chapter 4 - Type 1

Paragraph specifications   OK

Indents: Paragraph space: Cancel
  Left [0]   mm   Before [0]   mm
  First [0]   mm   After [0]   mm   Rules...
  Right [0]   mm   Spacing...

Alignment: [Left]   Dictionary: [US English]

Options:
  ☐ Keep lines together   ☐ Keep with next [0] lines
  ☐ Column break before   ☐ Widow control [0] lines
  ☐ Page break before   ☐ Orphan control [0] lines
  ☒ Include in table of contents

Options
Rulers   ⌘R
Snap to rulers   ⌘[
Zero lock

✓ Guides   ⌘J
✓ Snap to guides ⌘U
Lock guides
Column guides...

Autoflow

Index entry...   ⌘;
Show index...
Create index...
Create TOC...

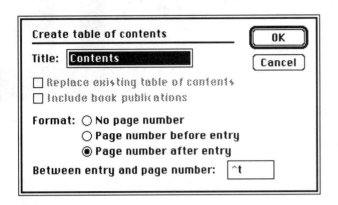

Figure 4. This is the *Create TOC* dialog box. The word *Contents* appears by default alongside the *Title.* line. This may be deleted and replaced with a title of your own, up to 30 characters in length.

Replace existing table of contents is only available for selection, if a previous contents has been generated. When available, it is automatically checked. It may be unchecked, if necessary, to allow you to compare old and new contents' versions.

Include book publications is only available if the publication is included in a *Book list.* When available, it is automatically checked. You may uncheck it, if you wish, to review contents for only a single publication.

The *Format* section of this dialog box allows you to choose *No page number,* or select between *Page number before entry* or *Page number after entry.* The bottom line, *Between entry and page number,* allows adjustment of the spacing between a contents heading and the various page numbers. The default format code is '^t' for a tab with dot leaders. Other codes may be used — these are listed in the PageMaker Reference Manual Appendix.

Clicking on OK in Figure 4 generates the table of contents. You may then place this as you do any text file in PageMaker.

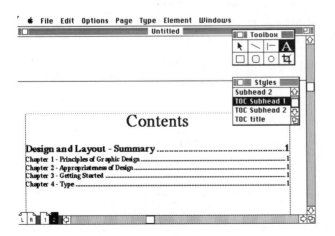

Figure 5. When the contents is generated, PageMaker automatically creates TOC styles, based on the styles of the original paragraph, but with the word TOC in front of them. TOC style fonts are Times Roman, by default. These TOC styles can be changed or edited in the same way as other paragraph styles.

INDEX GENERATION 14

CREATING INDEX ENTRIES

The *Index entry* command in the **Options** menu is used to identify words to be indexed within a publication. Before choosing this command, you need to do one of two things:

(a) create an insertion point in the text near to where you wish to reference a word, or;

(b) select a word using the text tool.

Figure 1. Once the *Index entry* command is then chosen, the *Create index entry* dialog box appears.

```
┌─────────────────────────────┐
│ Options                     │
├─────────────────────────────┤
│ ✓ Rulers              ⌘R    │
│   Snap to rulers      ⌘[    │
│   Zero lock                 │
├─────────────────────────────┤
│ ✓ Guides              ⌘J    │
│ ✓ Snap to guides      ⌘U    │
│   Lock guides               │
│   Column guides...          │
├─────────────────────────────┤
│   Autoflow                  │
├─────────────────────────────┤
│   Index entry...      ⌘;    │
│   Show index...             │
│   Create index...           │
│   Create TOC...             │
└─────────────────────────────┘
```

Figure 2. If you selected text, then this text will appear as shown here in the Level 1 *Topic:* box (Apples). If you created an insertion point, then the *Topic* levels will have no text in them. This latter method is used when you wish to insert a different word or phrase in the index, other than that contained in your text paragraph. You are then free to key in your own index word into the Level 1 *Topic:* rectangle. Notice the three different *Topic* levels available.

```
┌──────────────────────────────────────────────────────┐
│ Create index entry                          ┌──────┐ │
│                                             │  OK  │ │
│ Topic:                    Sort:             └──────┘ │
│ ┌──────────────┐ ┌─┐ ┌──────────────┐      ┌──────┐ │
│ │ Apples       │ │⇕│ │              │      │Cancel│ │
│ └──────────────┘ └─┘ └──────────────┘      └──────┘ │
│ ┌──────────────┐     ┌──────────────┐      ┌──────┐ │
│ │              │     │              │      │Topic.│ │
│ └──────────────┘     └──────────────┘      └──────┘ │
│ ┌──────────────┐     ┌──────────────┐      ┌──────┐ │
│ │              │     │              │      │H-ref │ │
│ └──────────────┘     └──────────────┘      └──────┘ │
│                                                      │
│ Range: ⦿ Current page                                │
│        ○ To next style change                        │
│        ○ To next occurrence of style: ┌─────────┐   │
│                                       │Body text│   │
│        ○ For next │1│ paragraphs      └─────────┘   │
│        ○ Cross-reference (H-ref)                     │
│                                                      │
│ Reference override: ☐ Bold ☐ Italic ☐ Underline     │
└──────────────────────────────────────────────────────┘
```

For further descriptions see Figure 3.

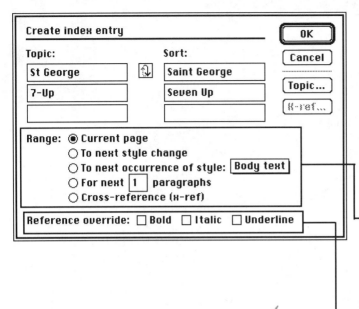

Figure 3. We now have entered both primary and secondary index entries. We have also entered additional information in the *Sort:* rectangles showing how we wish the *Topic:* index entries to be sorted. If you leave the *Sort:* rectangle blank, you may not get the alphabetic sequence desired, when dealing with items such as numbers.

The *Range* options allow you to decide how many pages to include for each index entry. The first four options are self-explanatory, the bottom option (*Cross-reference*) is discussed below.

The *Reference override* option allows you to change the type style, for emphasis on page numbers and cross referencing. The *Topic* and *X-ref* buttons are discussed below.

TOPIC AND CROSS-REFERENCING

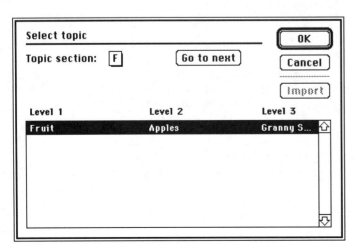

Figure 4. The *Select topic* dialog box can be entered by clicking on the *Topic* button in Figures 2 or 3. The *Select topic* dialog box allows you to select an index entry already included. This simplifies your work and reduces the possibility of misspelling subsequent entries of an existing index topic.

Figure 5. Cross-referencing to other index entries is done by first entering the word you wish to cross reference in the *Create index entry* dialog box. Here, 'Apples' is entered and it is to be cross-referenced to another entry, called 'Bananas' (e.g. Apples. *See* Bananas) . Choose *Cross-reference* towards the bottom of the dialog box, and then the *X-ref* button.

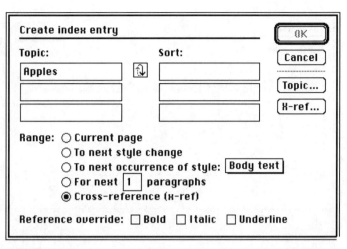

Figure 6. The actions of Figure 5 bring you to the *Select cross-reference topic* dialog box. In this box, find the 'Bananas' entry by selecting the 'B' alongside *Topic section,* or click on *Go to next* until 'Bananas', appears. Select 'Bananas' and click on OK. That brings you back to Figure 5. Click on OK once more to finish the operation.

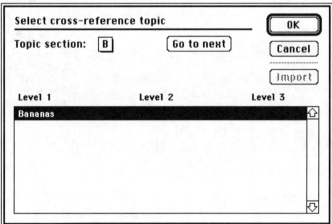

SHOW INDEX COMMAND

Figure 7. Select the *Show index* command to review all index entries before generating the index.

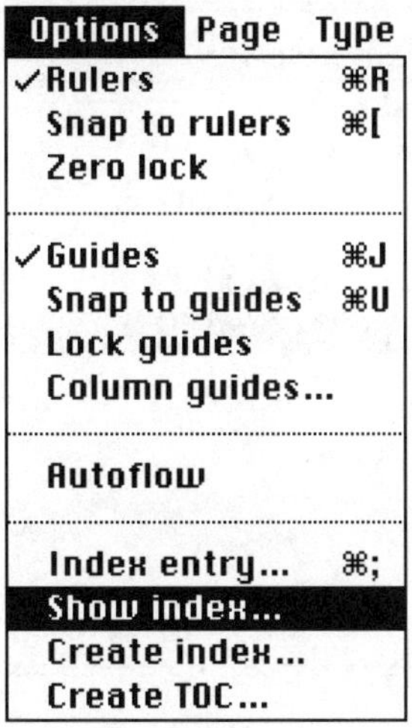

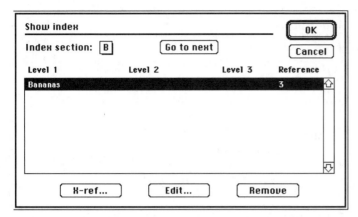

Figure 8. The *Show index* dialog box allows you to add *cross references*, *Edit* index entries or *Remove* entries. For example if you wish to cross reference 'Bananas' by adding the following:
'Bananas. *See also* Apples'
you would first find the 'Bananas' entry as shown in this figure. Then click on the *X-ref* button.

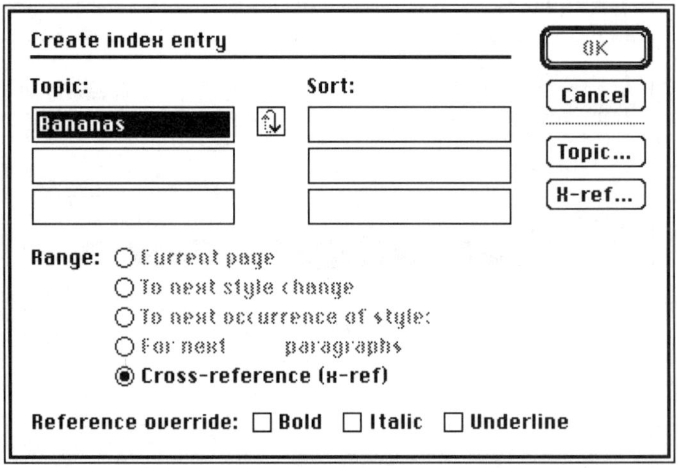

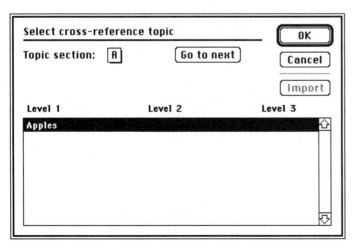

Figure 9. You then get the *Create index entry* dialog box. Click on the *X-ref* button to get the Figure 10 *Select cross-reference topic* dialog box.

Figure 10. 'Apples', starting with 'A', will come up first. It will already be highlighted; simply click on OK, twice, to get back to the *Show index* dialog box. Bananas will now be shown, cross-referenced to Apples (see Figure 11).

Figure 11. The *Show index* dialog box again, with the cross-referenced 'Bananas' entry.

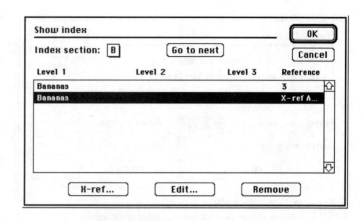

CREATING THE INDEX

Figure 12. The *Create index* command, from the **Options** menu, is used to finally create the index, once all index entries have been entered, cross-reference and edited as necessary. This causes the Figure 13 dialog box to appear.

Figure 13. The *Create index* dialog box. The default title as shown here is *Index*. You may delete this and include your own, to a maximum of 30 characters. *Replace existing index* is not checked if this is the first use of this command, otherwise it will be checked. Uncheck this if you wish to retain the existing index. *Include book publications* only applies if this current publication contains a book publication list. You may check this option if you want the full *Book list* index, or uncheck it if you only want the single publication index.

Clicking on OK would generate the index.

Clicking the *Format* button provides the Figure 14 *Index format* dialog box.

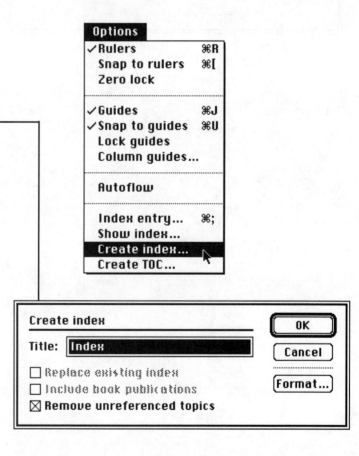

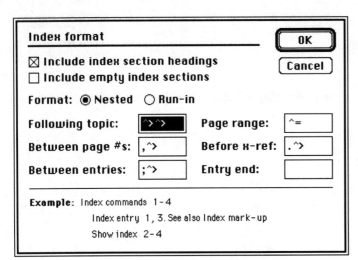

Figure 14. This is the *Index format* dialog box. You can choose to select or deselect the two top options at your own choice. The section headings refer to the A, B, C, etc. which occur at the beginning of each alphabetical section of the index. Examples of the format of *Nested* or *Run-in* are shown at the bottom of the dialog box, as you choose each option.

The remainder of this dialog box highlights the different characters used between index entries, page numbers etc. More details of these are in the PageMaker Reference Manual Appendix.

CREATING TABLES

ABOUT TABLE EDITOR

The Table Editor is a separate program to PageMaker. It enables you to set up tables then import them into PageMaker.

STARTING TABLE EDITOR

Figure 1. To start Table Editor, locate the Table Editor icon on the desktop, and double-click on it with your mouse.

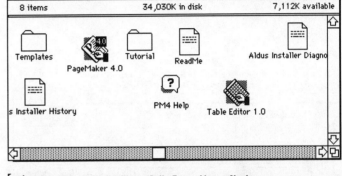

Figure 2. This is the initial menu bar you will encounter after activating the Table Editor icon with the mouse.

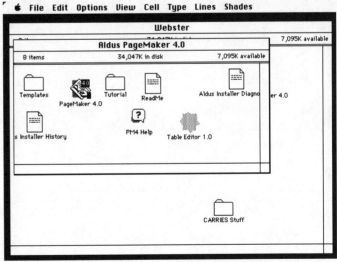

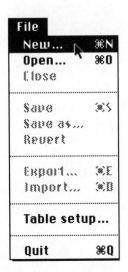

Figure 3. Activate the **File** menu with the mouse, and select either *New* for an untitled publication, or *Open* to open a previously saved document. We are selecting *New* in this Figure.

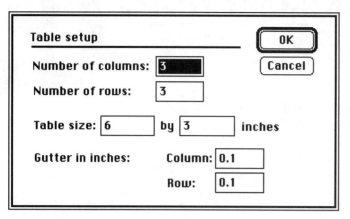

Figure 4. This is the *Table setup* dialog box that appears after selecting *New*. It is here that you initially define the number of columns and rows, and the size you would like your table to be. This can be modified at a later date, in a number of ways, including through the *Table setup* command in the **File** menu.

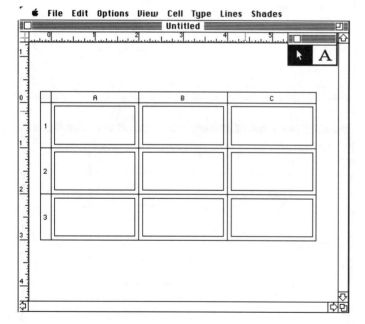

Figure 5. After selecting OK in the *Table setup* dialog box of Figure 4, this is how your initial table will look, with the default settings unchanged.

TYPING IN TEXT

Figure 6. To type in text, simply select the text tool, click the mouse inside the chosen cell, and start typing.

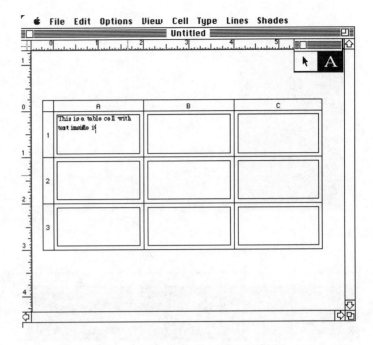

Figure 7. To move from cell to cell, when you are entering information into multiple cells, there are a number of methods:

(a) Use the Tab key to move to the right.

(b) Use the Shift + Tab keys to move to the left.

(c) Use the Return key to move downwards.

(d) Click the text cursor inside the chosen cell.

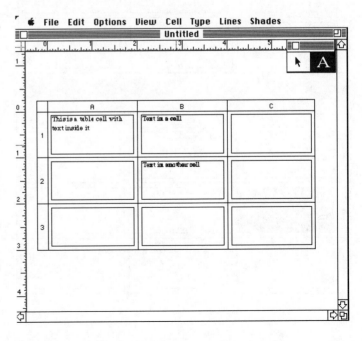

SELECTING CELLS

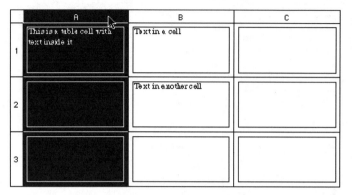

WITH THE POINTER TOOL

Figure 8. Select a whole column by clicking on its corresponding grid label letter, in this case A.

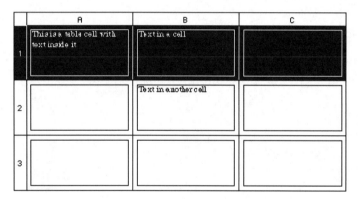

Figure 9. Select a whole row by clicking on its corresponding grid label number, in this case 1.

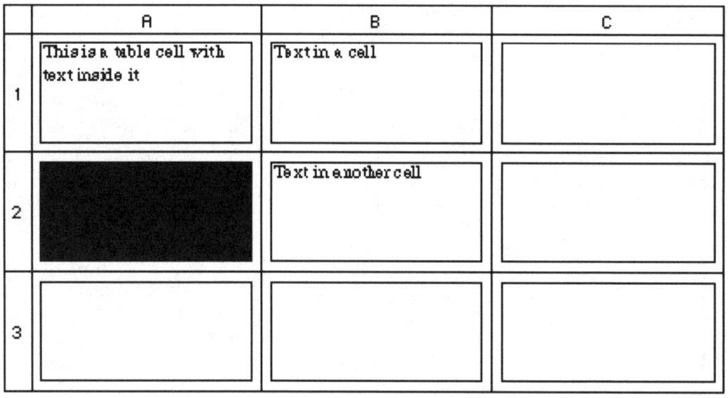

Figure 10. Individual cells are selected by clicking on the specific cell once with the mouse.

Figure 11. Multiple cells are selected by holding down the Shift key as you select the cells with the mouse, or dragging the mouse over the ones you wish to select.

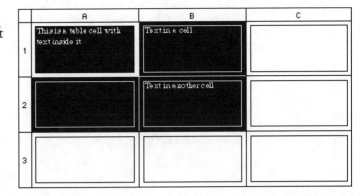

WITH THE TEXT TOOL

Figure 12. With the text tool, you may select individuals cells for formatting in a variety of ways. Simply inserting the cursor is enough to select a cell with the text tool.

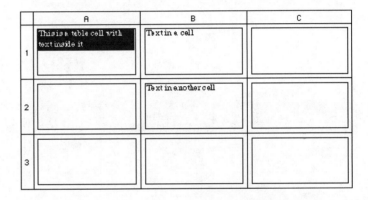

FORMATTING TEXT

Figure 13. To format text, it must first be selected. Once selected, you may apply any of the text formatting options from the **Type** menu, in the same way as you would within PageMaker. Here we are changing the point size of the selected text.

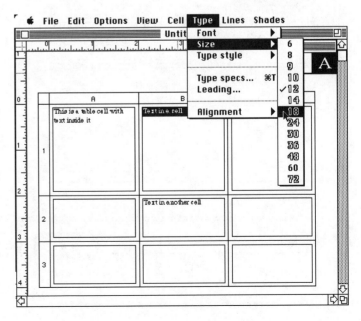

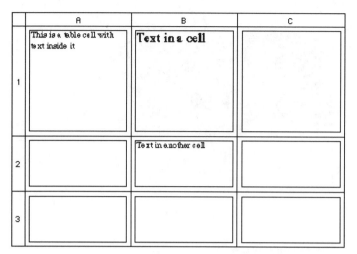

Figure 14. This shows the result of the change in point size.

Text may be selected with the text or pointer tools to change formatting attributes.

RESIZING ROWS AND COLUMNS

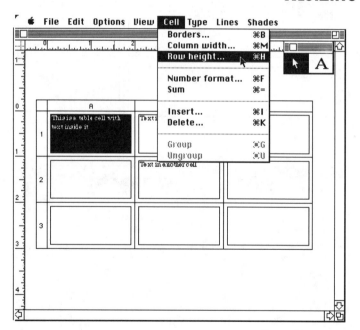

Figure 15. To change the height of a row, select a cell from that row, and then select the *Row height* command from the **Cell** menu.

The pointer or text tools can be used to select the initial cell.

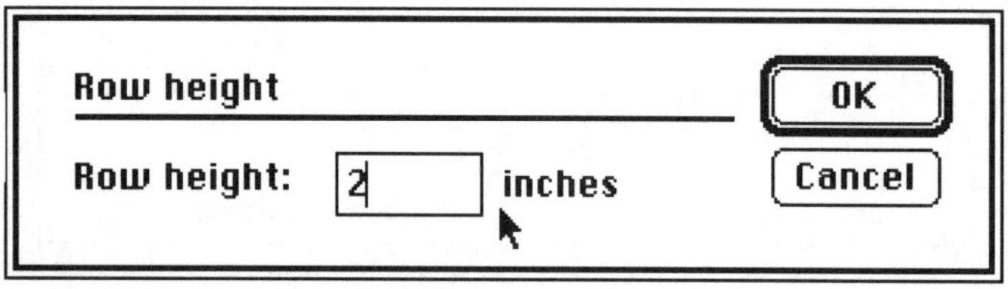

Figure 16. From Figure 15, the *Row height* dialog box is activated. We changed the initial setting to 2 inches and selected OK.

Figure 17. This is how the table now looks. You can change the width of columns using the same method as for rows, but choose *Column width* in Figure 15.

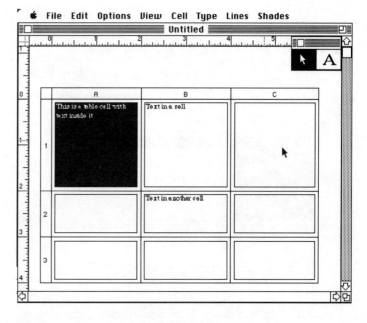

Figure 18. Rows or columns may be resized manually by placing the cursor between a column or row, as shown here, until a double-headed arrow appears. Hold the mouse down and move to a new position to resize the column (or row).

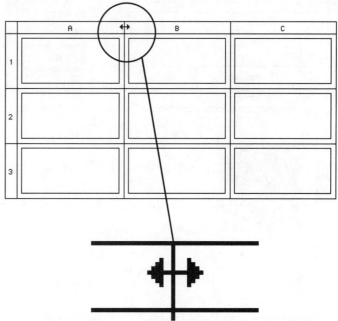

INSERTING ROWS AND COLUMNS

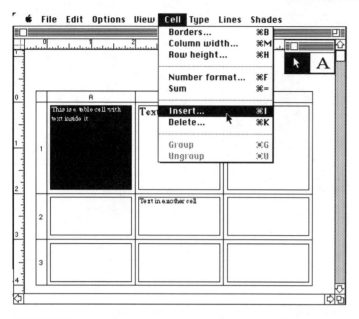

Figure 19. To insert a column or row, highlight a cell and then select the *Insert* command from the **Cell** menu.

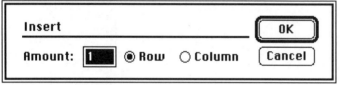

Figure 20. The *Insert* dialog box is activated. This is where you choose to insert either a column or a row. A new row will appear above the selected cell, and a new column will appear to the left of the selected cell.

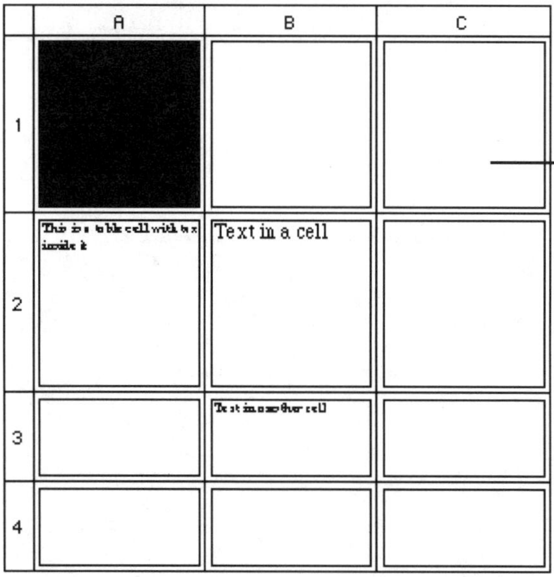

Figure 21. This is the row inserted from the actions of Figure 19.

You may also add rows and columns using the *Table setup* command from the **File** menu.

DELETING ROWS AND COLUMNS

Figure 22. To delete rows or columns, use the *Delete* command from the **Cell** menu in the same way as the *Insert* command is used.

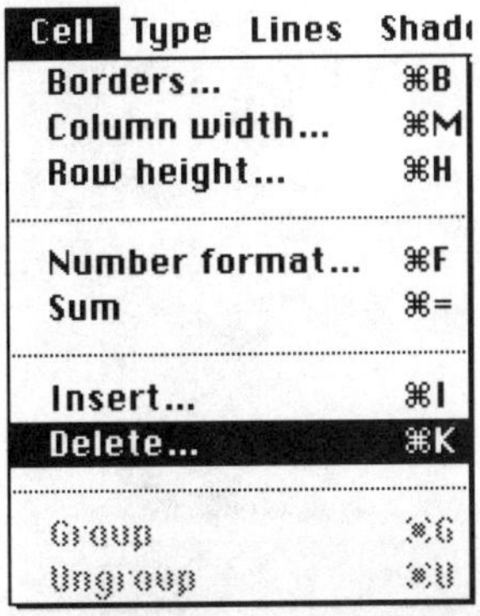

GROUPING CELLS

Figure 23. Cells are grouped together to create header rows of a table. Highlight the cells you wish to group together with the pointer tool, and select the *Group* command from the **Cell** menu.

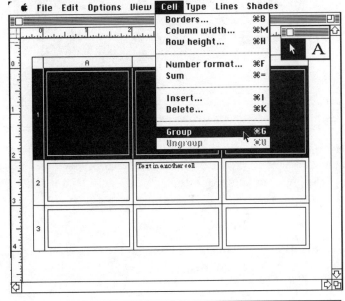

Figure 24. The result. The new larger cell is ready for text insertion.

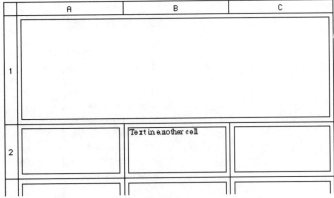

CHANGING LINE ATTRIBUTES

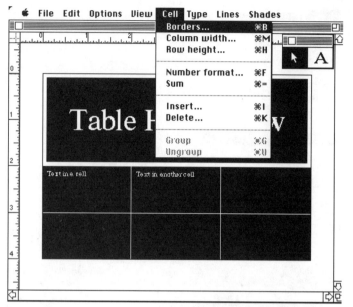

Figure 25. For this example of modifying line attributes, we turned the *Grid lines* and the *Grid labels* off in the **Options** menu.

To apply a different line thickness to the table, select the cell or cells required. We have the whole table selected. Select the *Borders* command from the **Cell** menu.

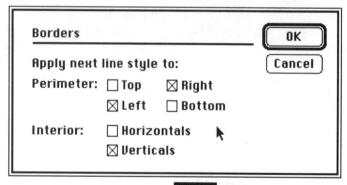

Figure 26. Deselect the lines you do NOT wish to change. We are going to apply a different line style to the interior vertical lines, and the exterior lines on the left and right of the table. Click on OK.

Figure 27. With the table still selected, select the line thickness from the **Lines** menu. We have selected *None.*

Figure 28. This is the result of changes made from Figures 25 through 27.

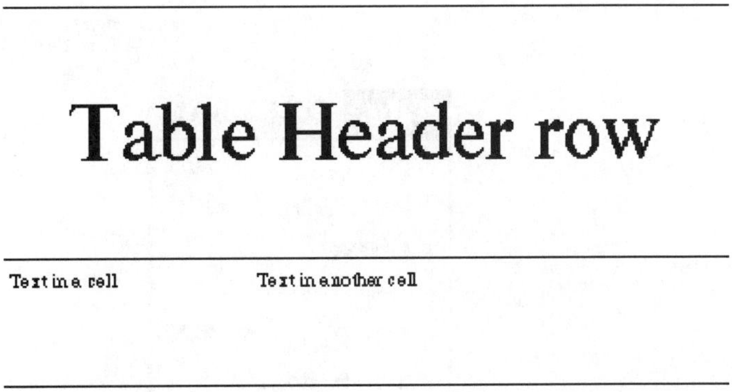

Table Header row
Text in a cell
Text in another cell

APPLYING SHADES

Figure 29. To shade a cell or cells, first select the required section of the table. Activate the **Shades** menu and select the desired shade.

File Edit Options View Cell Type Lines Shades
Untitled
None
Solid
10%
20%
30%
40%
60%
80%
Table Header row
Text in a cell
Text in another cell

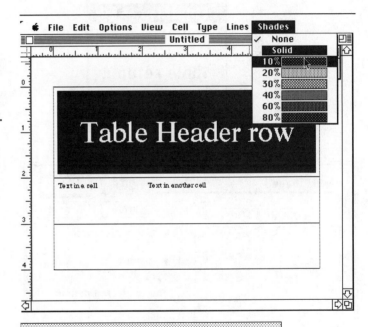

Figure 30. From the operation of Figure 29, the top row now has a 10% shade.

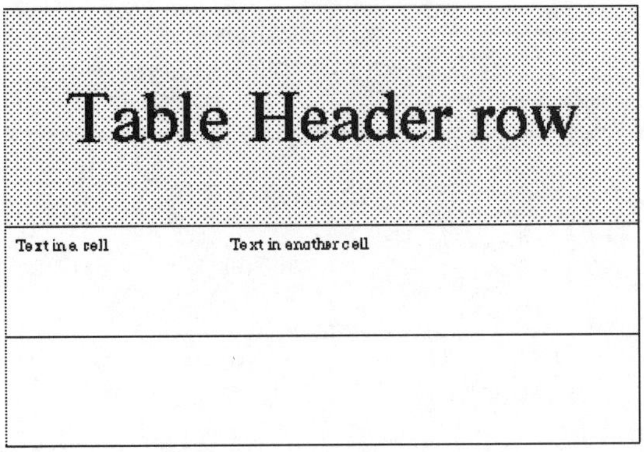

Table Header row
Text in a cell
Text in another cell

EXPORTING FILES FROM TABLE EDITOR

Figure 31. In order to bring files into PageMaker, you need to first export the table file out of Table Editor. Select the *Export* command from the **File** menu to activate the *Export to file* dialog box.

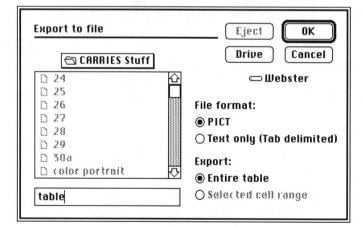

Figure 32. Here you must select a *File format* option. If you select the *Text only* option, only the table text within the cells will be exported as a text file. PICT format will allow you to import the table into PageMaker as a graphics file.

You may also export parts of the table, after selecting the desired section of the table with the mouse, and choosing the Selected cell range option.

Name your file after you have selected the required options, and click on OK. This file will then be written to disk, which will not be apparent until you go to place it into PageMaker.

IMPORTING FILES INTO PAGEMAKER

Figure 33. After completing the procedure described in Figures 31 and 32, open the PageMaker file in which you wish to place the table.

Use the **Place** command to place the file on the page.

Alternatively, you may use the *Import* command from the *story editor* mode.

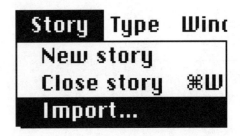

Figure 34. This is how a typical table file will look in PageMaker, when saved as a PICT file.

Because it is a graphic, it can be resized, moved and cropped in exactly the same way as you would any graphic.

Table Editor files may also be copied to the clipboard, and then pasted directly into a PageMaker publication.

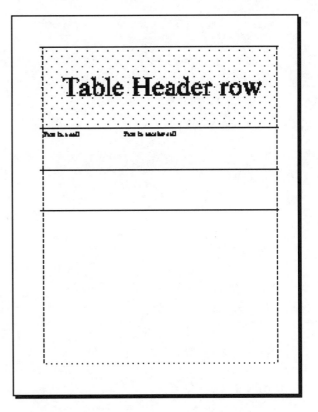

MENU SUMMARIES 16

File

New...	⌘N
Open...	⌘O
Close	
Save	⌘S
Save as...	
Revert	
Export...	
Place...	⌘D
Links...	⌘=
Book...	
Page setup...	
Print...	⌘P
Quit	⌘Q

Edit

Undo	⌘Z
Cut	⌘X
Copy	⌘C
Paste	⌘V
Clear	
Select all	⌘A
Find...	⌘8
Find next	⌘,
Change...	⌘9
Spelling...	⌘L
Show clipboard	
Preferences...	
Edit layout	⌘E

Options

✓Rulers	⌘R
Snap to rulers	⌘[
Zero lock	
✓Guides	⌘J
✓Snap to guides	⌘U
Lock guides	
Column guides...	
Autoflow	
Index entry...	⌘;
Show index...	
Create index...	
Create TOC...	

Page

✓Fit in window	⌘W
25% size	⌘0
50% size	⌘5
75% size	⌘7
Actual size	⌘1
200% size	⌘2
400% size	⌘4
Go to page...	⌘G
Insert pages...	
Remove pages...	
✓Display master items	
Copy master guides	

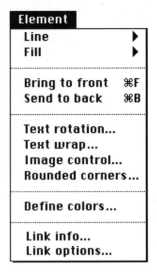

Type

Font	▶
Size	▶
Leading	▶
Set width	▶
Track	▶
Type style	▶
Type specs...	⌘T
Paragraph...	⌘M
Indents/tabs...	⌘I
Hyphenation...	⌘H
Alignment	▶
Style	▶
Define styles...	⌘3

Element

Line	▶
Fill	▶
Bring to front	⌘F
Send to back	⌘B
Text rotation...	
Text wrap...	
Image control...	
Rounded corners...	
Define colors...	
Link info...	
Link options...	

Windows

Help...	
✓Toolbox	⌘6
✓Scroll bars	
✓Style palette	⌘Y
✓Color palette	⌘K
Untitled	
URGENT NOTICE!!:1	

GENERAL

Some commands have shortcut keys which perform the same function as selecting the command from the menu. The shortcut keys are shown to the right of the command in the menu.

Commands that have three dots after them activate a dialog box when the command is selected.

When a command has a check next to it, this means the command is currently activated.

A right facing arrow to the right of a command indicates that an additional sub-menu will appear, when this command is selected. The sub-menu commands can be activated by moving the mouse to the right, and then up or down the sub-menu.

```
┌─────────────────────┐
│ File                │
├─────────────────────┤
│ New...        ⌘N    │
│ Open...       ⌘O    │
│ Close               │
│ ·················   │
│ Save          ⌘S    │
│ Save as...          │
└─────────────────────┘
```

THE FILE MENU

The *New* command is used every time you start a new PageMaker document. It activates the *Page setup* dialog box, where you set the attributes for how the page layout of the document will look.

The *Open* command gives you access to all PageMaker files that have been previously saved on your hard disk or other disk drives. This is done by scrolling through the files and folders in the *Open* publication dialog box.

This command closes the current publication you are working on, but will not take you out of PageMaker. If you have made any changes to the current publication, you will be asked if you want to save the changes. If you select *Yes*, your changes will be saved. If you have not saved at all, you will be confronted with the *Save as* dialog box, where you give the document a name and decide where to save it. Once you have closed a PageMaker document, you are able to open another immediately by selecting the *Open* command.

The *Save* command saves your work. On selecting this command for the first time, you will activate the *Save as* dialog box, where you give the PageMaker document a name and decide where to save it. Once the publication is named,   you can then use this command without activating the *Save as* dialog box; your work will be saved directly into your named publication.

This command is used if you want to initially name your publication, or rename it. The *Save as* dialog box will once again be activated. This command can also be used to conserve memory. By saving a document in the same place and with the same name, it will take up less memory if you have recently edited it.

The *Revert* command returns the document to the state it was before you last saved it.

Text in PageMaker, whether it was created in PageMaker or a word processing program, can be exported to outside programs for editing. This command will let you export selected text to anywhere on your Macintosh in a number of formats. This is done through the *Export* dialog box activated by this command.

Use the *Place* command to bring text and/or graphics into a PageMaker document. On selecting this command, you will get the *Place document* dialog box. From this dialog box, you can scroll through the Macintosh's hard disk or external drives to locate the appropriate text or graphics.

The *Links* command activates the *Links* dialog box. This dialog box gives you information on the status of any text or graphics files you have linked to outside programs that originally created them.

The *Book* command lets you join several PageMaker documents together to create one long document. This allows you to create a table of contents and index that include all the linked documents. It also allows you to print all connected documents without opening each one separately.

The *Page setup* command activates the same dialog box you get when selecting the *New* command. Here you can make any necessary changes to the current layout and size of the document you are working on.

Use this command to get a hard copy of your PageMaker document.

Select the *Quit* command to leave PageMaker. If you have made any changes since last saving, or haven't saved yet, you will be asked if you want to save your work. If you choose to save the current document, you will be confronted with the *Save as* dialog box, if your publication is unnamed.

Edit	
Undo copy	⌘Z
Cut	⌘X
Copy	⌘C
Paste	⌘V
Clear	
Select all	⌘A
Find...	⌘8
Find next	⌘,
Change...	⌘9
Spelling...	⌘L
Show clipboard	
Preferences...	
Edit story	⌘E

Edit	
Undo	⌘Z
Cut	⌘X
Copy	⌘C
Paste	⌘V
Clear	
Select all	⌘A
Find...	⌘8
Find next	⌘,
Change...	⌘9
Spelling...	⌘L
Show clipboard	
Preferences...	
Edit layout	⌘E

THE EDIT MENU

Note: The edit menu on the right is applicable when working in the story editor. Note that some edit functions will not work when the story editor is not active.

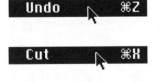

The *Undo* command will deactivates the last change you made to your document.

The *Cut* command will remove the selected text and/or graphics on your page, and place it in the clipboard.

The *Copy* command will place a copy of the selected text and/or graphic into the clipboard.

Once you have cut or copied text and/or graphics from the page, they will be saved in the clipboard until you paste them back into the document. Anything that's been cut or copied can be pasted back as many times as you require, or until another copied or cut object takes its place.

The *Clear* command will delete selected text blocks and/or graphics from the page, without placing them in the Clipboard. It works the same way as the *Delete* key.

If you are currently working with the pointer tool, and you choose this command, everything on the current page will become selected. If the text tool is currently active, and you want to use the *Select all* command, the cursor must be placed somewhere within the text you want to select. Once this is done and you choose this command, all text that is part of the same text file will be highlighted in reverse video.

Select all ⌘A

This command is used when in *story editor* mode. You place a specific word in the associated dialog box, and PageMaker will search for it.

Find... ⌘8

Once the word is found, the *Find* button will change to the *Find next* button and the *Find next* command will be highlighted in the **Edit** menu. Once PageMaker has found the word, it is possible to change its attributes.

Find next ⌘,

This command lets you search for a word in *story editor* mode and replace it with another word, or change its attributes.

Change... ⌘9

This activates PageMaker's spell check feature. The whole document, or selected text, will be scanned for spelling mistakes. This only works in *story editor* mode.

Spelling... ⌘L

Selecting this command shows whatever text and/or graphics you last cut or copied to the clipboard.

Show clipboard

This command activates the *Preferences* dialog box. This box lets you change the current measurement system which, in turn, affects everything that requires measurements in your publication, including the rulers.

Preferences...

When you are in *layout mode*, this command will appear as *Edit story*. It allows you to move to the story editor from layout view.

Edit story ⌘E

This command is activated to exit from the *story editor*.

Edit layout ⌘E

```
┌──────────────────────────┐
│ Options                  │
│ ✓Rulers            ⌘R    │
│  Snap to rulers    ⌘[    │
│  Zero lock               │
│ ·························· │
│ ✓Guides            ⌘J    │
│ ✓Snap to guides    ⌘U    │
│  Lock guides             │
│  Column guides...        │
│ ·························· │
│  Autoflow                │
│ ·························· │
│  Index entry...    ⌘;    │
│  Show index...           │
│  Create index...         │
│  Create TOC...           │
└──────────────────────────┘
```

THE OPTIONS MENU

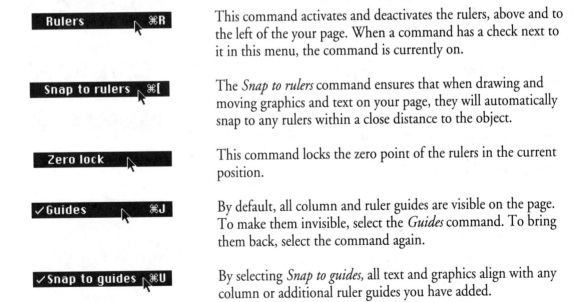

This command activates and deactivates the rulers, above and to the left of the your page. When a command has a check next to it in this menu, the command is currently on.

The *Snap to rulers* command ensures that when drawing and moving graphics and text on your page, they will automatically snap to any rulers within a close distance to the object.

This command locks the zero point of the rulers in the current position.

By default, all column and ruler guides are visible on the page. To make them invisible, select the *Guides* command. To bring them back, select the command again.

By selecting *Snap to guides,* all text and graphics align with any column or additional ruler guides you have added.

The *Lock guides* command locks all ruler and column guides in their current position. They can only be moved by selecting this option again.

Select this command to change the number of columns on your page and the space between columns. The *Column guides* dialog box will be activated, which also gives you the option of setting the left and right pages separately.

Column guides...

The *Autoflow* command determines how text is placed in your document. By default, this option will not be selected, therefore text will flow into your document as you place it manually. If *Autoflow* is selected, the text will flow until it runs out. The text flow icon will also change once Autoflow is selected.

Autoflow

The *Index entry* command, and associated dialog box, is for creating topic references and entries for the current publication's index.

Index entry... ⌘;

This command lets you check and make any necessary changes to the index entries before the index is generated.

Show index...

On selecting this command, the *Create index* dialog box appears. This command is used once you have created all index entries and made any necessary alterations. After clicking OK in this dialog box, the generated index can be placed into your document.

Create index...

The *Create TOC* command is used to generate a table of contents. The headings that appear in the table of contents are first specified in the *Paragraph specifications* dialog box. Once the table of contents has been generated, it can be placed in your document like any other text, and can be edited once it's been placed.

Create TOC...

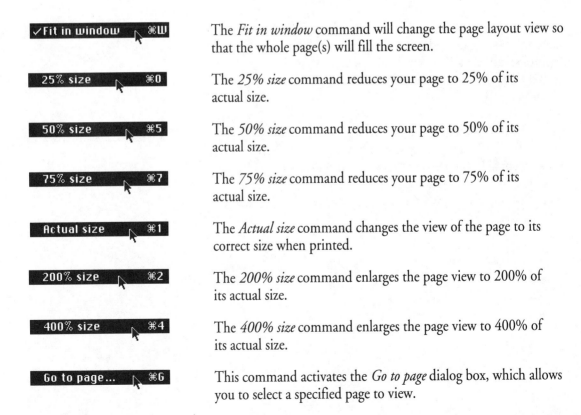

THE PAGE MENU

The *Fit in window* command will change the page layout view so that the whole page(s) will fill the screen.

The *25% size* command reduces your page to 25% of its actual size.

The *50% size* command reduces your page to 50% of its actual size.

The *75% size* command reduces your page to 75% of its actual size.

The *Actual size* command changes the view of the page to its correct size when printed.

The *200% size* command enlarges the page view to 200% of its actual size.

The *400% size* command enlarges the page view to 400% of its actual size.

This command activates the *Go to page* dialog box, which allows you to select a specified page to view.

The *Insert pages* command lets you place extra pages in the current document through its associated dialog box. You have a choice of placing the page in front, behind, or between the current page(s).

Insert pages...

The *Remove pages* command allows you to remove unnecessary or blank pages.

Remove pages...

By default, any text or graphics you have on the master pages will appear on all other pages. If you deselect this option, the master page items will not appear on the current page.

✓Display master items

Column and ruler guides placed on the master pages can be moved on all other pages. If you have moved them and want them to return to their original position, select the *Copy master guides* command.

Copy master guides

Type	
Font	▶
Size	▶
Leading	▶
Set width	▶
Track	▶
Type style	▶
Type specs...	⌘T
Paragraph...	⌘M
Indents/tabs...	⌘I
Hyphenation...	⌘H
Alignment	▶
Style	▶
Define styles...	⌘3

THE TYPE MENU

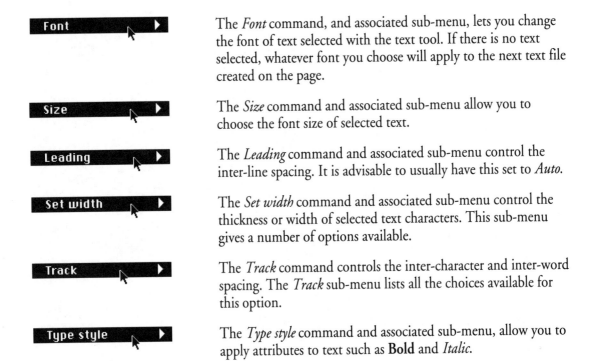

The *Font* command, and associated sub-menu, lets you change the font of text selected with the text tool. If there is no text selected, whatever font you choose will apply to the next text file created on the page.

The *Size* command and associated sub-menu allow you to choose the font size of selected text.

The *Leading* command and associated sub-menu control the inter-line spacing. It is advisable to usually have this set to *Auto*.

The *Set width* command and associated sub-menu control the thickness or width of selected text characters. This sub-menu gives a number of options available.

The *Track* command controls the inter-character and inter-word spacing. The *Track* sub-menu lists all the choices available for this option.

The *Type style* command and associated sub-menu, allow you to apply attributes to text such as **Bold** and *Italic*.

The *Type specs* command activates the *Type specifications* dialog box. This dialog box gives you the option of modifying all the previous six commands within one dialog box. As well, you can also change the color, case and position of selected text.

Type specs...   ⌘T

The *Paragraph* command activates the *Paragraph specifications* dialog box. From here you can change and control the attributes associated with the selected paragraphs, such as spacing, alignment, and indenting.

Paragraph...   ⌘M

The *Indents/tabs* command allows you to set up indents, and a variety of different tabs, which will apply to any text that is selected.

Indents/tabs...   ⌘I

The *Hyphenation* command controls the number, type and position of hyphenations in your text.

Hyphenation...   ⌘H

The *Alignment* command and associated sub-menu let you quickly change the alignment of selected text, without having to go through the *Paragraph* command dialog box.

Alignment   ▶

The *Style* command lets you apply a style to a selected paragraph, or one you are about to create. The list of styles available in this sub-menu are default styles that come with PageMaker, and/or the styles you have created through the *Define styles* dialog box.

Style   ▶

The *Define styles* command activates the *Define styles* dialog box. Here you are able to save a set of attributes under a chosen name. The same attributes can then be applied to multiple paragraphs, without wasting time choosing the numerous paragraph commands.

Define styles...   ⌘3

Element

Line	▶
Fill	▶
Bring to front	⌘F
Send to back	⌘B
Text rotation...	
Text wrap...	
Image control...	
Rounded corners...	
Define colors...	
Link info...	
Link options...	

THE ELEMENT MENU

The *Line* command and associated sub-menu allow you to apply different line thicknesses and styles to graphics created in PageMaker.

The *Fill* command and associated sub-menu allow you to apply a range of different shades and patterns to graphics created within PageMaker.

The *Bring to front* command places whatever object you have selected, with the pointer tool, to the front of the screen, so it will sit on top of all other objects or text.

The *Send to back* command is opposite to the *Bring to front* command. Any graphic or text selected with the pointer tool, when this option is activated, sits behind all other text and/or graphics on your page.

Any text block selected with the pointer tool can be rotated in 90 degree increments. This is done by choosing the *Text rotation* command, and selecting the degree of rotation from the *Text rotation* dialog box .

The *Text wrap* option controls an invisible border around a selected graphic, so that all text will flow around the graphic. A number of different choices are available. If there is currently no graphic selected, the text wrap will apply to the next graphic placed or created.

Text wrap...

This command applies to imported graphics, such as scanned images. The lightness and contrast of a selected graphic can be altered through the dialog box activated with this command.

Image control...

The *Rounded corners* command, and associated dialog box, allow you to vary the corner radius of the rounded-corner graphics drawing tool.

Rounded corners

The *Define colors* command lets you create and modify colors found in the *Color palette,* which can then be applied to objects and text.

Define colors...

The *Link info* command activates the *Link info* dialog box. This command can only be activated when a graphic or text block is selected. It supplies you with information regarding graphics or text that have been created externally, and which are still linked to these outside programs. Linked graphics and text created in external programs can be linked to the PageMaker file, so that any changes you make in the outside programs will be reflected in PageMaker.

Link info...

The *Link options* command and dialog box allow you to choose which method to apply when linking a particular document.

Link options...

Windows

 Help...

 ✓Toolbox   ⌘6
 ✓Scroll bars
 ✓Style palette   ⌘Y
 ✓Color palette   ⌘K

 Untitled

THE WINDOWS MENU

The *Help* command activates a how-to-use PageMaker dialog box. Every command and a range of applications are explained.

The *Toolbox* command activates and deactivates the toolbox. By default, the toolbox is always visible when you start a new PageMaker file, and because it is constantly used, it normally stays on. If you do not want it on screen, select the *Toolbox* command and it will disappear.

By default, the *Scroll bars* are always on, but can be turned off by selecting this command.

The *Style palette* is activated by selecting the *Style palette* command. It will appear on screen below the toolbox, and can be deactivated by selecting this same command. It is used to apply styles to selected paragraphs; styles that have been created in the *Define styles* dialog box.

The *Color palette*, like the *Style palette*, is activated and deactivated by selecting this command. It contains the default colors that come with PageMaker, and any colors you may have created through the *Define colors* dialog box. The *Color palette* sits below the *Style palette* and is used for applying the colors to selected text and/or graphics.

This *Untitled* command in the **Windows** menu is the name of the currently open PageMaker document, which is obviously still untitled. It allows you to move between *story editor* and your actual working page. This is done by selecting the current File name displayed in the menu.

KEYBOARD SHORTCUTS

Desired result	Keyboard shortcut
Move to next page	*Command + Tab*
Move to previous page	*Command + Shift + Tab*
Move page in any direction	*Option, and drag*
Move page horizontally or vertically	*Option + Shift, and drag*
Resize a graphic in correct proportions	*With the mouse held down on any handle, press the Shift key*
Change a rectangle created in PageMaker to a square	*With the mouse held down on any handle, press the Shift key*
Change an oval created in PageMaker to a circle	*With the mouse held down on any handle, press the Shift key*
Resize a paint-type graphic to its correct proportion, so it fits the resolution of your printer	*Command + Shift and mouse held down on any handle*
Discretionary hyphen	*Command + -*
Em dash (—)	*Option + Shift + -*
En dash (-)	*Option + -*
Opening double quotation mark (")	*Option + [*

Desired result	Keyboard shortcut
Closing double quotation mark (")	*Option + Shift + [*
Opening single quotation mark (')	*Option +]*
Closing single quotation mark (')	*Option + Shift +]*
Master page number markers (LM, RM)	*Command + Option + P*
Bullet (•)	*Option + 8*
Registered trademark (®)	*Option + R*
Trademark (™)	*Option + 2*
Copyright (©)	*Option + G*
Paragraph marker (¶)	*Option + 7*
Section marker (§)	*Option + 6*
Em space	*Command + Shift + M*
En space	*Command + Shift + N*
Fixed space	*Option + space bar*
Make selected text one point smaller	*Option + Command + Shift +,*
To make selected text one point bigger	*Option + Command + Shift +.*
To make text Bold	*Command + Shift + B*
To make text Italic	*Command + Shift + I*
To give text an Outline	*Command + Shift + D*

Desired result	Keyboard shortcut
To give text a Shadow	*Command + Shift + W*
To make text Small caps	*Command + Shift + H*
To make text All caps	*Command + Shift + K*
To make text Subscript	*Command + Shift + -*
To make text Superscript	*Command + Shift + =*
To Underline text	*Command + Shift + U*
To Left align text	*Command + Shift + L*
To Right align text	*Command + Shift + R*
To Center text	*Command + Shift + C*
To Justify text	*Command + Shift + J*
To Force Justify text	*Command + Shift + F*

Index

More from Peachpit Press...

Canned Art: Clip Art for the Macintosh, 2nd Edition
Erfert Fenton and Christine Morrissett
A sample book showing over 15,000 pieces of clip art available from 35,000 different companies. The two optional All Star Sample Disks contain 61 pieces of clip art. *(650 pages)*

Canvas 3.0: The Book
Deke McClelland
The first guide to Deneba's newly enhanced drawing and painting program. *(373 pages)*

Desktop Publisher's Survival Kit
David Blatner
Essential tips and tools for setting up a desktop publishing system. Includes a disk containing 12 great desktop publishing utilities, two PostScript fonts, and 450K of clip art. *(426 pages plus disk)*

Desktop Publishing Secrets
Robin Eckhardt, Bob Weibel, and Ted Nace
Hundreds of the best desktop publishing tips from five years of *Publish* magazine. *(550 pages)*

EcoLinking
Don Rittner
The first guide to how we can use computer networks, bulletin boards, and online services to access environmental information. *(300 pages)*

Illustrator Illuminated
Clay Andres
Detailed case studies of seven actual illustration projects created in Adobe Illustrator. Full color throughout. *(200 pages)*

The Little Mac Book, 2nd Edition
Robin Williams and Kay Yarborough Nelson
Peachpit's bestselling beginner's guide to the Macintosh, updated for System 7. *(184 pages)*

The Little Mac Word Book
Helmut Kobler
The essential features of the new Microsoft Word 5.0, clearly explained and indexed. *(240 pages)*

The Little QuicKeys Book
Steve Roth and Don Sellers
A handy guide to CE Software's QuicKeys 2.0 macro program. *(268 pages)*

The Little System 7 Book
Kay Yarborough Nelson
Teach yourself the essentials of System 7 and skip the technical mumbo jumbo! *(160 pages)*

The Macintosh Font Book, 2nd Edition
Erfert Fenton
Everything from font basics to resolving ID conflicts—the definitive guide to Mac fonts. *(348 pages)*

The Mac is not a typewriter
Robin Williams
Twenty easy tips for producing beautiful typography with a Mac and a laser printer. *(72 pages)*

The Macintosh Bible, 3rd Edition
Sharon Aker (edited by Arthur Naiman)
The bestselling Mac book ever, with over 600,000 copies in print *(1,115 pages)*

PageMaker 4: An Easy Desk Reference
Robin Williams
A reference book that lets you look up how to do specific tasks with PageMaker 4. *(784 pages)*

The QuarkXPress Book, 2nd Edition
David Blatner and Keith Stimely
Peachpit's bestselling, comprehensive guide to QuarkXPress and XTensions, now updated for version 3.1. *(640 pages)*

Real World FreeHand 3
Olav Martin Kvern
An insider's guide to the latest release of this popular Mac drawing program. *(474 pages)*

Order Form

(800) 283-9444 or (510) 548-4393
(510) 548-5991 fax

#	Title	Price	Total
	Canned Art: Clip Art for the Macintosh	29.95	
	Canvas 3.0: The Book	21.95	
	Desktop Publisher's Survival Kit (with disk)	22.95	
	Desktop Publishing Secrets	27.95	
	EcoLinking	18.95	
	Illustrator Illuminated	24.95	
	The Little Mac Book, 2nd Edition	14.95	
	The Little Mac Word Book	15.95	
	The Little QuicKeys Book	18.95	
	The Little System 7 Book	12.95	
	The Macintosh Font Book, 2nd Edition	23.95	
	The Mac is not a typewriter	9.95	
	The Macintosh Bible, 3rd Edition	28.00	
	PageMaker 4: An Easy Desk Reference (Mac Edition)	29.95	
	PageMaker 4: Visual QuickStart Guide (Mac Edition)	12.95	
	The QuarkXPress Book, 2nd Edition	27.95	
	Real World FreeHand 3	27.95	

Tax of 8.25% applies to California residents only.
UPS ground shipping: $4 for first item,
  $1 each additional.
UPS 2nd day air: $7 for first item, $2 each additional.
Air mail to Canada: $6 for first item, $4 each additional.
Air mail overseas: $14 each item.

Subtotal	
8.25% Tax (CA only)	
Shipping	
TOTAL	

Name		
Company		
Address		
City	State	Zip
Phone	Fax	
❏ Check enclosed	❏ Visa	❏ MasterCard
Company purchase order #		
Credit card #	Expiration Date	

Peachpit Press, Inc. • 2414 Sixth Street • Berkeley, CA • 94710
Your satisfaction is guaranteed or your money will be cheerfully refunded!